# Contents

Acknowledgments     xi

Foreword     xv

Introduction     1

**Part I:** Effective Members

Working Together     7

An Organization Is People—Bringing in Newcomers     10

Successful Publicity     15

Successful Programs     24

Managing One's Life     40

**Part II:** Effective Organization Business

Wolfe's Rules of Order     55

Raising Money     70

Elections     78

Officers and Directors     84

Why Reinvent the Wheel?     91

**Part III:** Effective Leaders

So You've Been Chosen As Our Leader     103

Keeping Committees Alive and Well     111

Board Meetings     117

Afterword     124

Appendix — Or     127

Bibliography     139

To
Will, John, and Peter

"The Americans of all ages, all conditions and all dispositions constantly form associations. They have not only commercial and manufacturing companies in which all take part but associations of a thousand other kinds, religious, moral, serious, futile, restricted, enormous, or diminutive. The Americans make associations to give entertainments, to found establishments for education, to send missionaries to the antipodes. Wherever at the head of some new undertaking you see the government of France or a man of rank in England, in the United States you will be sure to find an association."

*Alexis de Tocqueville*
*1805–1859*

# Acknowledgments

SO MANY PEOPLE are responsible for whatever insights this book offers that space precludes naming them all. I can only give my inadequate public thanks to the people most directly involved, and hope to thank everyone personally over the next many years.

First, I am forever grateful to my parents, Mary Lou and William Luedders. They were my inspiration and my models long before this book took form, and they inspired and helped as the book progressed.

I also acknowledge my debt to the members of Audubon, the League of Women Voters, the PTA, the Michigan Natural Resources Commission, and the numerous other community, church and environmental groups from whom I acquired most of my organizational experience and knowledge. Two individuals must be named: Norma Raby, an organizational leader of national repute, was my chief source of advice for many years; furthermore, her willingness to work on a host of unglamorous tasks during numerous crises ensured successes we might never have had. And I wish I could tell Arleen Sweet how much her support, enthusiasm and encouragement meant to me; she lives on in the hearts of all the Audubon members who knew her.

William J. Mullendore edited most of the manuscript throughout the several years I worked on this book. His own volunteer experiences added an important dimension to his editing. I deeply appreciate his wise counsel and professional help.

Elsie Green Ostergard also deserves special mention and thanks. Elsie is another volunteer who was always available in a pinch. She also typed—and retyped—my manuscript, with never a complaint for the many times I changed my mind. Thanks, too, to Peg Daniel and the rest of the staff and volunteers at the West Michigan Environmental Action Council for their cheer, encouragement, advice and patience.

This book contains fewer errors and better ideas because countless individuals gave me useful suggestions. I am especially grateful to the people who reviewed all or part of my manuscript and commented at length. George Bruso, Ann Cooper, Pat Davis, Henry Erb, Diane Lobbestael, John Bartlow Martin, Edward Post, and Daniel Spalink served as my experts (among others I've named elsewhere) for specific chapters. Sarah and Robert Dawson, Mary Jane Dockeray, Frank Dutten, Helen Elliott, Shirley Eyler, Gwen Hibbard, David Jenkins, Lee Ann Lipke, Dean Luedders, Helen Maher, Frances Martin, Ditty Smith, and Hilary Snell also offered ideas that became important additions in this book.

My thanks go, too, to still others from whom I received advice and help. June Bieszka, Christine Byron, Diane Casey, Gilbert Davis, Gerald Elliot, Nelle, Don and Margaret Frisch, John McGarry, Kate Moody, David Richey, Joseph Rink, Margaret Sellers, James Sanderson, Joan Saub, Karen Scott and Harry and Betty Whiteley.

If this book is clear, much credit must go to Catherine Orgill West and Dr. Lamar Janey, from my Hollins College days. Unique roles were also played by Byron Kennard, and by Nancy Jack Todd, Gary Hirschberg, and my son John, at New Alchemy Institute. It is hard to give proper acknowledgment. Three other people responded to my requests for counsel and help with such unexpected generosity that I owe them a debt I can never repay. My inadequate thanks go to Dennis Meadows, John G. Mitchell, and Werner Veit for their time, initiative, and help.

I am deeply grateful, of course, to Russ Peterson for writing the Foreword. All who know of his tremendous dedication and experience in public service will understand how proud I am to have his words begin this book.

I also acknowledge my admiration and appreciation for the people with Brick House: publisher Jack Howell, Tamara Stock, Jim Bright, Mike Fender, and Joyce Thompson, and all the rest of the Brick House crew. Their expertise, enthusiasm, support and flair have made the experience of getting published a delightful and satisfying adventure.

Finally, a deep bow to the people who were closest to this project for all too many years—my husband, Willard, and our sons, Peter and John. Aside from their role as my sounding board, both Peter and John went over the final draft of the manuscript and gave me their detailed, written suggestions for changes and additions. Will was my constant source for help and advice. He never complained (well, almost never) about the cost to his sanity or our bank account, and he accepted with grace and cooperation my frequent need to work alone at our cabin. My family's help and good humored tolerance made all the difference, and they have my love and everlasting gratitude.

# Foreword

## by Russell W. Peterson

WHEN ENTHUSIASTIC AND civic-minded volunteers get together to save a park or raise funds to build a new hospital wing, they very often don't realize what is involved. They should be reminded, at the outset, that they will need tools like organization charts and bylaws. These tools will save them countless hours by spelling out a rational division of duties and line of responsibility. But they should also be reminded that in real life those little boxes on the chart are human beings. One of them may have a headful of good ideas and boundless enthusiasm but have to be sat on from time to time, being carried away by an idea that turns out to be a real klinker. Another may be unquestionably the most knowledgeable member of the committee, but have an abrasive personality that puts his colleagues off. A third isn't particularly smart or talented but is so hard working, self-effacing, and dedicated that it's almost embarrassing to the rest of the committee. These people and the rest of the crew face the challenge of learning to work together successfully. The other people they will have to work with, both among the membership and in the outside community, will be equally full of human strengths and weaknesses.

They should be reminded, yes. But scared off? Of course not. They should be encouraged and reassured as they set out on their new project. Millions of other Americans have done it. In fact, America relies heavily on volunteers, their communities and their country need them. The work can be rewarding; the reason so many volunteers keep coming back for further service is that it's satisfying. To use a word that appears more than once in Joan Wolfe's book, volunteer organizations can, and should, be fun.

So volunteers tackling a new job need warnings and need encouragement. The great thing about this book is the way the two are balanced. Joan Wolfe's infectious enthusiasm is convincing proof that volunteering can be both rewarding and fun. At the same time she provides the volunteer with a common-sense how-to book that pulls no punches about the pitfalls—the needless mistakes—that can lead to failure. There are checklists of details that are surprisingly often overlooked. For example, everything the new volunteer would need to know to plan a meeting is here, from advice on dealing with projection equipment to methods of introducing a speaker.

Most important, she somehow manages to draw a clear distinction between "handling" people and "working with people." That can sometimes be a rather thin line, and it is perhaps the most important thing Joan Wolfe has to say. Our friend with the abrasive personality has an important contribution to make to the committee. Mrs. Wolfe believes that the key to bringing out such contributions is teamwork guided by tact, understanding, flexibility, and as much firmness as is necessary.

I've been discussing this book in terms of its value to volunteer workers, because that's the audience it is written for. But I should add that in my time I've sat through numerous hours of staff, board, and organizational meetings in a big corporation, a state capitol, and Washington, D.C., and I know that volunteers aren't the only ones who will learn something from *Making Things Happen*.

If every organization picked up just a few helpful hints from this book, just think what the national total would be in terms of frustrations avoided, wheels not spun needlessly, and effectiveness increased!

RUSSELL W. PETERSON
*President*
National Audubon Society

# Making Things Happen

# Introduction

CLUBS AND OTHER voluntary organizations make a rich contribution to American life. Most of us want to be involved; we join, participate in, and lead organizations to share hobbies, serve our communities, or change the world according to our interests and our vision. This book is to make that participation more enjoyable, and more effective.

For me, association with such groups began early. Family life often revolved around my parents' activities in hospital and church groups, PTA, Scouts and school boards, Red Cross and business associations.

Because my parents were intensely interested in the causes they served, they advised each other on how to deal with people or institutional difficulties to get each problem solved and each job done. I grew up appreciating the importance of activities outside one's household and work place, and understanding that we can learn ways to become more effective in our efforts.

My adult life, and that of my husband, has been one of participation as an organization member; I am committed to the belief that some of society's needs are filled only if a volunteer fills them, that many important changes will be made in the world only if people give their time freely to tackle the problems.

Regardless of what the job is, doing things right counts. To be effective, we must do things well. I believe

1

strongly in what organizations can do for their own members and for the larger community. I also believe that volunteers are not nearly as effective as they could be for the time and effort they expend. Members of clubs and other organizations do countless jobs they aren't trained for: working with and leading other members (which is a lot different from working with people who are paid to cooperate), introducing a speaker, conducting a meeting, raising money, publicizing an event.

Too often, volunteers play by ear. We repeat each other's mistakes. We need advice. We live in an age in which we can't afford the wasted time, frustrations and misunderstandings that are too often a part of organization life. More than ever, club members insist that their time be productive and personally worthwhile.

That is what this book is all about. It is to help you become more effective in your own efforts. It is to make your club or other voluntary organization successful. This book tells you how to publicize your events, how to run a meeting, how to treat your speakers. It offers ideas to keep hardworking members and to bring out the talents of introverted ones. It tells you how to manage your own competing priorities so that volunteerism doesn't become an intolerable burden.

I write from hard-won experience. As a volunteer I've participated in many, many ways: from baking cookies for the PTA, to being its president; from addressing envelopes, to writing hearing statements; from collecting for the United Fund, to organizing a major environmental council; from serving on local committees, to chairing local and statewide organizations; from building bluebird houses, to leading the successful passage of a model state Environmental Protection Act. I've lost sleep and suffered from my failures, and I've been awarded and honored for my successes.

Whatever the work, I've known that if the issues were worthy, the less glamorous tasks were as important as the seemingly more significant jobs. But they all would have been much, much easier if we had known more before we started.

Before I get into the details of what I learned that may help you, I think it is important to suggest some general principles. Hence, some thoughts to guide you:

My first principle is: Work with your fellow members, don't drag them. Move together to get the job done. We can take a lesson from experienced lifeguards who, unlike many would-be rescuers, do not use all their strength trying to drag a thrashing, terrified person to safety. Too many "rescuers" have drowned with their victims. Instead, the lifeguard rolls with the victim, slowly moving out of trouble, into safety. Like the lifeguard, we must deal with people as they are, instead of as we want them to be. People have their own needs, strengths and weaknesses, and their own ideas. When everybody participates in the decisions, everybody wins.

A second principle is: If we expect people working under our leadership to put in a real effort, we have to work at least as hard as they do. No one likes to feel he or she is being used.

A third principle: Appreciate and show your enthusiasm for the efforts of others. The steering wheel is useless without all the other parts of the machine.

And, a word of encouragement: No matter how well you work, make schedules or delegate tasks, even the best plans sometimes go awry. This book isn't meant to be one more yardstick for the conscientious person to measure against.

A wise minister I know points out that it is very human to take our failures and look at them, dissect them in bed at night, roll them over and over like a dog plays with a bone, bury them and dig them up to examine them all over again. But what do we do with our victories? We say, "Oh well, that was just doing my job!" How easily we dismiss our victories.

How much better it would be if we remembered what Charlie Brown said when told that we win a few and we lose a few. Charlie's reply was, "Gee, that would be great." We might also remember much older advice. "The only people who never make a mistake are the people who do nothing." So, may this book help you be philosophical about your failures, but may you also enjoy each opportunity to do well, and *appreciate* your victories.

As you work toward accomplishing your goals, may your world go more smoothly, your organization be more effective, and everyone have more fun making his contribution.

# Part I:

# Effective Members

# Working Together

ACTIVE GROUPS HAVE goals, and members must help achieve those goals. Unfortunately, egos do get in the way, jealousies do arise, and petty differences sometimes interfere.

You can't do much about changing the personalities of other members. You can, however, avoid fussing about other people's shortcomings. Anyone who declines to be critical of fellow members is an asset to the group.

You can also avoid fretting over whether you get credit for an idea or accomplishment. I was once a member of a committee chaired by an outrageous egotist. We all recognized that if we wanted to get anything done, we would have to deal with his jealousies and conceit; there certainly was no way we could change him. Therefore, we gave him our ideas privately, worked hard, and then presented him with our results so he could announce them as if they were his own. That required commitment and some swallowing of our pride, but by zeroing in on what we wanted to accomplish, we overcame our frustrations and enjoyed a successful year.

We all have egos, and those egos too often get in our way when we want to get something done or an idea across. We have to learn how to deal with this. One way is to avoid overwhelming others with our own good suggestions. Take it easy! If you think you know best what should be done, remember that other people may not agree. Deciding that something is right neither makes it right nor makes others concur. And like the unsuccessful "rescuer" in my introduction, if you try to pull others along too quickly, you fail.

When you have an idea, plant some seeds. Distribute carefully chosen literature, or throw out the idea casually and see how it flies. One way to plant or test an idea is to form it into a question or into a tentative comment: "Should we think about the possibility . . ." or, "I wonder if it would be effective if we . . ." or, "Professor Diltz has suggested that . . ."

If there is little enthusiasm, continue to educate. If your idea will require a vote, make sure you have done your homework. Talk to individual members, find out what their concerns are, and meet those concerns with answers. If you feel strongly about something important to you, and want a positive vote, don't bring it to a head until you are sure you have the votes. It is easier to keep educating and gathering support than it is to start over again after being voted down.

When you are working on anything, remember the old rhyme about the motorist who was "right, dead right." Some people enjoy being martyrs ("I told you so"), but it isn't a rational position. It is better to learn how to be right and succeed than to be right and fail. Learning to put a brake on your enthusiasm or distress when you don't have the group with you, learning to quietly educate, learning to be patient when you feel that something cries out for attention, is absolutely required. Don't ever assume that everyone else agrees with you. My greatest surprises and defeats have occurred when I thought something was self-evident, and then nobody agreed!

It is natural to have special friends in a group, but lean over backward to avoid forming a clique. Go out of your way to pay attention to the people who appear less exciting to you; seek out people outside your own circle of friends. The more you get to know other people, the more you will come to appreciate them.

Some of the most unassuming or seemingly unattrac-

tive people have unusual gifts, interests, knowledge or wis-
dom that can enrich your life and that of your organization. You can be the one who brings out those untapped
talents and personalities. Broaden your life to include the
unprepossessing people around you, and you will be in for
some great—as well as humbling—surprises.

# An Organization Is People — Bringing in Newcomers

**A**N ORGANIZATION IS people. *People* work toward the organization's goals; *people* with enthusiasm and dedication to those goals make the organization succeed. That enthusiasm and dedication come from a constant infusion of new blood into the group—the new volunteers who aren't weary from past efforts and who haven't run out of fresh ideas. Every successful volunteer organization knows the importance of new members.

Some organizations do a horrible job of attracting new people. They miss great opportunities to obtain badly needed human resources by not making a special effort to make people feel welcome and wanted. As newcomers, most of us have had the terrifying experience of walking into a room full of strangers standing in tight circles. There seems to be nothing much one can do except stand alone and feel stupid—or run.

For anyone who finds himself in the uncomfortable position of being the outsider, however, there are ways to cope: If all the people standing in tight circles are too much to overcome, act in the most natural way you know how; stand or sit in your most relaxed pose and wait until the program begins or someone speaks to you. (You may want to die while you're waiting, but that will pass.) If you can find someone to approach, you say, "Hello, I'm Orwell Finkblossom. This is my first meeting here." If you are really unlucky, the other person will give a mere, surprised "Oh." Gulp three times, smile your most courageous smile, and ask a question to save the day. Remember that it is the rare human being who is really a snob; the "oh" answer just means that the other person doesn't know how to act.

You may have to try more than once, but in any case, when you get someone's attention, you can talk about how you happened to learn about the group, why the program looked interesting, how surprised you are at the large group, or any other positive or complimentary comment that may elicit a response and start a conversation. A little thought beforehand regarding the nature of the organization and why you want to attend the meeting will give you clues for conversation. Comments about yourself, your experiences in a similar group, and questions about the group always help. A real icebreaker might be that you are new in the community (or are free from past commitments) and are trying to find where you are needed most. If you don't arouse some interest after really trying, you should find another group.

Groups who really want new members and new workers should not let this happen. If the organization wants to survive, the real burden is on the members. Most newcomers aren't willing to keep bravely forging ahead time after time until somebody encourages them to participate. We all join groups in which we feel most welcome.

There are many reasons why organizations are less than the friendly groups they picture themselves to be. It's much more comfortable for members just to keep on getting along with the old gang. Also, most people lack know-how in making newcomers feel comfortable. Members themselves feel shy, and it isn't easy to walk up to a stranger and begin a conversation. It's a lot easier to talk to people you know, and most of us have trouble overcoming our own insecurities long enough to think about somebody else. A group has to work hard to overcome this very human problem.

A first necessity is for the members to recognize just how important this matter really is. Group members who complain—and it's a frequent complaint—that people are selfish with their time and won't participate are probably forgetting that if the members did a better job of making new people feel welcome, newcomers might fall all over themselves in their eagerness to participate. Organization leaders must make a determined effort to overcome the problem of welcoming new members, preferably by appointing a greeting committee or membership chairperson, and by making sure the job is carried out. The designated committee chairperson should not forget the following responsibilities:

1. Someone should be assigned to bring a wide felt pen and name tags. Pleasant persons with nice smiles should be asked to sit at a table by the door and give out name tags. At least one of these people should also know how to write names clearly *in big block letters* so the tags can be easily read. Too many people just can't bring themselves to write their own names legibly and large enough so other people can read them. A different color tag for newcomers, incidentally, helps identify them. Some organizations have special tags for everyone at each meeting, or they have permanent name tags for members. It's not important how it's done, as long as it is done. Even in small groups, if people don't know each other well, name tags are a big help toward getting to know one another. (This avoids those embarrassing situations when we don't remember the names of the persons we've already met twice.)

2. Members should be continually reminded to look out for new faces.

3. Your most relaxed, gregarious members should be appointed to be at the door. Their job is to go up to all new faces, introduce themselves, and help people get acquainted. Same advice for the newcomers, of course, applies to these greeters: "I'm Jane Doe and I haven't met

you yet." Or in case of doubt, "I'm not sure that I've met you. Do you come here often?" Barbara Walters' book, *How to Talk With Practically Anybody About Practically Anything* (see the Bibliography), is full of great advice.

A newcomer appreciates being told who people are as well as something about the organization. It doesn't hurt, either, to babble on about one's own interests if it helps keep the conversation going.

4. Someone must be responsible for refreshments. Refreshments are an inducement for people to stand around and talk, and so help members and newcomers get to know each other. Refreshments also help in other ways: they offer something to sip while thinking of what to say, people at the refreshments table to exchange a few words with, and a place to go when finding oneself alone wondering what to do next.

5. One of the membership committee functions should be to make follow-up calls to any newcomers. This is genuine evidence of your organization's interest, and gives the newcomer the opportunity to ask additional questions and get better acquainted.

A lively organization may want to combine the refreshment, hospitality and membership functions as subcommittees of the membership committee. If these groups meet together at the beginning and middle of the year, new plans are likely to come from the free exchange of ideas, and all will be more conscious of the importance of what they are doing.

It is always a help to have your program and business meeting start immediately. This gives new people the opportunity to come in and sit down shortly after arrival and find out something about the group. Once the newcomers sit through the program or business, there is common ground for conversation, and the first-timers can begin to feel a part of the organization. In any case, it is the responsibility of the membership or hospitality committee to keep their eyes open and seek out new people (and shyer members) who are standing alone in a corner hoping for a friendly face to appear.

Another aid to full participation is to make sure that everyone feels a part of the proceedings. In a large organization the president should always introduce himself or herself and everyone else at the head table (except the speaker, who will be introduced later). Whenever the president calls on anyone to give a report, there should be a real introduction, not just a cozy, "Sam, let's hear from you now," but rather, "Now I'd like to call on Sam Smith, our hard-working finance chairperson." Make it as clear as possible to new people and guests just who everyone is and what's going on.

Finally, in any organization where volunteers are needed and prospective workers are present, the president should continually make a warm plea for suggestions and help. Let people know they are needed and wanted. Only new blood and ideas keep an organization a good one. The president's job is to keep the program lively and ongoing. In turn, members must cooperate with the president. When it comes to staying alive and growing, an organization usually deserves—through its efforts or lack of effort—just exactly what it gets.

# Successful
# Publicity

**A**H! PUBLICITY! TALK to the members of almost any organization and they will tell you they don't get the publicity they deserve. But few groups understand how to interest the news media, and innocents make mistakes that actually damage their relations with the media. Your responsibility in seeking publicity, therefore, is to learn how to do it right.

Your first step must be to understand the problems of the news media: lack of time, space and reporters to cover all the subjects which could be covered. You've got to learn not to expect top-rate coverage for tenth-rate news. That is hard, especially if you have expended a lot of effort. The next step is to learn the most effective ways to provide news for the media. And you've got to learn how to make it really interesting. Sometimes for example, just a small change in plans—a bit of pizzazz which would help make a good picture—can make your bazaar different enough to be considered news.

Though you may have real news, on first blush it may not seem very special to a reporter. Make sure the reporter understands the importance of what you are doing. For instance, you plan to bring a speaker of international significance, but the speaker is little known to the reporter. The standard résumé from your speaker's office may lack the information to suggest that the speaker will convey noteworthy ideas.

15

Don't ever assume that the reporter knows your subject as well as you do. Make sure that you add the needed information in your news release; or call the press, TV and radio stations and give them background. Point out that Dr. Sedem Bugleys is not just a professor at Egghead University, who founded the Center for the Study of Parasitic Hymenoptera. Add that Dr. Bugleys is the man who set the scientific world spinning by his efforts in the Amazon to save the great striped jungle ant from extinction because he believes it holds a key to man's warlike behavior. That way, you are more likely to spark some interest. You may not only get a bigger story ahead of time (which will help bring out your audience) but also increase your chances of reporters interviewing the speaker or covering the talk.

Realize that chance is always a factor in getting news. If your bazaar (jazzed up and complete with your minister riding a donkey up the church steps) falls on the day after a hurricane, your story may be squeezed out. If news is slow and your event seems more interesting than whatever else is on the news desk that day, you may be in luck.

There are guidelines that will help you predict what kind of publicity you might get. Those guidelines are based on the following questions:

1. Is the public invited? If so, be sure to include this information in your news release. If not, your event is of little interest to the public, and therefore to the media, as a news item *ahead* of the event. (It may, however, be of some interest after it has happened.)

2. Is the event very different from that of many other groups? If not, don't expect anything more than a few lines in the newspaper, and you may not even get that. Some newspapers list organization events. If your newspaper doesn't, you might suggest it. People looking for something to do can look there for ideas, and the paper can make a lot of groups very happy.

3. If you are bringing a speaker, is he or she the sub-

ject of special interest? Is his subject new, or of current concern, or is he or she an expert? If the speaker is local, is there something about him or her that commands special respect?

4. Are you doing something unusual which can draw attention, even though the event itself lacks news value? A note of caution, here, however: there is a limit to ideas that truly make an event newsworthy. Ministers on donkeys, helium-filled balloons carrying baskets of children, and other new or oddball ideas rarely interest the media. Special themes and unusual activities will indeed attract more people to your event, but they still may be boring news. Do what you can to attract attention, but remember how many events go on all the time in most cities, and be philosophical when you are disappointed. Remember, too, that the size of your city and the number of events going on at the same time will have a lot to do with the amount of coverage given to your organization's project.

Some organizations, such as environmental groups, can become important sources of general or technical expertise to news reporters. This kind of help to the media cements a relationship and keeps a reporter interested, so that the chances of an organization having its information heard and used are greatly increased. It doesn't insure a story every time; remember that no matter how good your relationships, a reporter won't write a story if it isn't newsworthy. But good relationships will increase the chances of stories helpful to the organization's point of view, even if the news isn't directly related to the organization. The key to becoming such a source is to provide accurate, sound information. Getting honest, straightforward facts from an organization builds trust, and trust based on credibility is the key to any relationship a reporter has with an organization.

Organizations can help the media and build trust by opening their libraries and encouraging their own experts to be available to reporters. They can further their own cause by tipping reporters off to news they become aware of, even if they haven't the time or interest to become involved. Such a relationship cannot develop to everyone's mutual benefit if the group's information is weak, tainted by emotion, or faulty in any way.

With those guidelines and thoughts in mind, let's proceed with the work of getting publicity. If the publicity chairman will get a committee together at the beginning of the year, the work can be spread among the members.

Activities and planning by the committee will become another good way to get to know one another. Among the jobs which should be discussed, and to which different committee members may be assigned for special functions, are:

1.  Writing the press release and getting it to the newspaper's city editor (or editor, depending on the size of your community).

2.  Sending your information to individuals and groups who might be interested enough in your project to publicize it to others or to their own members. These "support" groups can be very effective in publicizing your information. Be sure to suggest to them exactly what you hope they will do for you, such as printing your information in their newsletters or announcing it to their members.

3.  Making posters and distributing them. If the subject is of special interest, a local school might help.

4.  Sending postcards, with the information clearly and fully typed or printed, to all local radio stations. Most will use the information if it is sent three weeks in advance. If the stations' policies aren't known to your group, someone should call to find out what the procedures and policies are.

5.  Trying to get your president, a committee chairperson, or most interesting and articulate member, on local radio and TV talk shows. If you have an out-of-town speaker, stations may be receptive to the suggestion of an interview ahead of the program or after the program, if the speaker's schedule permits and the speaker is willing.

6. Talking up your special function at your own meetings and in your own newsletter.

### Releasing Your News

An organization should try to make it easy for the media to use its material. With news of consequence, it is very, very important to announce it so that all the media will have a chance to use the information on the same day. If you break your news so that an afternoon paper can print it the day before the competing morning paper, or the evening TV and radio stations can announce it the day before the newspapers can report it, you are likely to have an indifferent newspaper on your hands, and perhaps an angry reporter. An even worse mistake is to give the news to some of the media and not the rest. You are going to have to be sure to remember everybody, and then time your release very carefully.

This means you must find out ahead of time just when news deadlines are. Even though your news isn't of such great significance that it must be released so carefully, you will want it to reach as many people as possible. Check with your local media for their recommendations regarding the best times to get news to them, so that your news will be (you hope) published at certain times. All the media have deadlines; they will be happy to advise you.

Remember, however, that no matter how well you try to plan, your news will be covered (*if* it is covered) at the time which fits the media's needs best. You are going to this trouble not because you will necessarily succeed, but because you will have the best chance of succeeding if you do things right.

Make sure that someone calls the city editors of the newspapers, and news directors of local TV and radio, and discusses these questions with them. Find out when the best time is to talk to them. Always ask when you call whether you have caught them at a bad time. Don't be alarmed if they are gruff or snap at you. Some newspeople fancy themselves as hard-bitten, but most don't; they are just very busy at some times during the day. All newspeople appreciate courtesy, honesty, fairness, accuracy and an understanding of the difference between an ordinary function and an activity of broad interest.

Even if you believe you have major news, my advice is, don't hold a press conference. If you do, it is possible no one will show up. The press conference is usually limited to *very important people* in very large cities.

Instead, keep in mind the rule for letting everyone get out the news about the same time. If you hope for a television interview, call or deliver the news to the stations early enough to give them the opportunity to ask you to appear on TV. At the same time, make sure they understand why you consider the event of special significance.

Usually the best method for announcing your news is through a press release. This can be hand-delivered if necessary to assure receipt at the right time. There are rules for writing a good release; if you follow them, you are more likely to get the attention you seek. A news release insures more accurate reporting and improves the likelihood the story gets used. If you know a particular reporter you would like to have cover the story, take or send the release directly to that reporter in the hope that he or she will be able to cover it. Otherwise, someone with less interest or knowledge about the subject may be assigned, and you may not be as happy with the way the subject is handled.

A good news release helps reporters do their job. The information they most need is all there, already written. Remember the daily time pressures on the media. Follow the example at the end of the chapter, and you will know you have done a proper job. Note that a release tells when the news may be used. (To be on the safe side, never release a big news story early, depending on everyone to respect your time schedule.) The release also should tell where a reporter may call for more information.

Type on organization stationery, if possible, and

double- or triple-space your story. If there is more than one page, type "more" at the bottom and number the pages. Type on only one side of each page. Clean your typewriter, type neatly, and don't use an old typewriter ribbon. Make copies for each of the media and for your files. With local libraries and even grocery stores providing copy machine service these days, good copies are now easy and inexpensive to obtain.

Use a headline to give quick notice about the topic. Then write the story as a reporter might write it. Remember to cover the "*who, what, where, when, how* and *why*" at the beginning. You aren't writing a suspense novel; you are providing news.

Memorize those five w's; they are important for any hearing statement, letter to the editor, letter to a public official, or report to members. No matter how many times you send out information, include the basic facts each time. If your story is cut, or a reader doesn't finish the story, the essentials will remain. Read news stories for examples of the kind of writing you will imitate. If your story is rewritten—and it probably will be—don't worry about it as long as the facts are correct.

Remember that imagination and courtesy, and a positive, realistic understanding of what is *news* will go a long way toward getting attention when you really want it. For example, if many awards are given for local efforts, your newspaper or television stations may no longer consider them worthy of pictures (the standard scene of the award-givers handing out a large plaque, for instance). What you can do is to time your presentation to coincide with a special function where the media are more likely to be present and where the award could get some mention along with the story about the event.

Remember too, that newspeople have many demands on their time and attention. Do you want them to attend a special event? Send a personal note about the function well ahead of time and advise them what will admit them. Individuals may not accept a lunch or dinner invitation, although ethical standards differ; early on you should ask that question along with others regarding deadlines and media policy. Realize that you probably will not get a commitment from a reporter (something may suddenly break elsewhere), so it is best to go no further than calling to give a last-minute reminder.

After all your hard work, you still may fail to make the news the way you expected or hoped. Getting angry is a waste of energy. Try to figure out what you may have done wrong, or whether the news was as exciting as you thought it was. You might call a newsperson and ask for advice or suggestions, but don't become a pest. Often it will not have been your fault; your news just got cut because something else was more important that day. With all news, luck plays a major part.

Organizations sometimes feel that because one group made the news one day theirs should be given equal treatment later. There is no way, however, for reporters and editors to keep track of whom they covered when. That is simply not the way they operate. If you work to understand these matters, always looking at your problem from the media point of view, you will ultimately succeed.

Finally, keep in mind the most important point: The best way to get attention, assuming you are publicizing your news properly, is to *DO SOMETHING IMPORTANT.*

**(An example of the first page of a news release.)**

# ENVIRONMENTAL COALITION

22 WEST MAIN ST., ALLEN WOODS, MICH. 49999

## NEWS RELEASE

October 1, 1980
For Immediate Release

Contact: Mary Jones
Energy Chairperson
Home: 444-3292
Office: 444-4222

### ENVIRONMENTAL COALITION OFFERS ENERGY CONSERVATION TOUR

(Who)    The Environmental Coalition today announced a tour of
(What)  homes for anyone interested in saving energy. "All homes on the
(Why)  tour were chosen because they can offer energy saving ideas to
other home owners," said Mary Jones, the Coalition's energy
chairperson.

(When)    The tour will begin at 9 a.m. Saturday, October 21, and will
(Where)  start from the Smith Building. Buses will be provided. Donation
(How)  is $5.00, and the public is invited.

The tour climaxes the Coalition's year-long search for Allen
County residents who use effective methods to save energy and
cut down on their fuel and electric bills.

"We deeply appreciate the cooperation of the homeowners
who have so generously agreed to open their homes to show
the public their creative solutions," Ms. Jones said. "This is a real
contribution to others in our county."

She warned that not all the energy-saving homes on the tour
will be unique. Some were chosen as outstanding examples of
simple but effective remodeling. Others are examples of the creative use of technology, such as solar and wind power.

"Probably most interesting is the underground home designed and built by the Carl and Elizabeth Weinstein family,

**(more)**

# Successful
# Programs

GOOD PROGRAMS ATTRACT and educate members. They are the result of good speakers and good audiences. You need both. This chapter will discuss how to attract and please them.

First, I don't know how people get the idea that speakers are dying for the opportunity to appear. If they're worth hearing, they lead busy, productive lives, and their visit to your group requires a sacrifice in precious time. They speak because their position and status require it, or because they believe they have something important to say. While they may receive many small satisfactions from speaking, giving a talk requires preparation, time, and a strain on the nervous system. Organizations that treat their speakers with appreciation and understanding keep alive for all organizations the prospect of continuing to have good programs.

Your responsibility to a potential speaker is to define your requirements, expectations and conditions exactly. Your guest needs to get agreement on topic, on length of program, and even a good notion of attendance. A talk before 20 people is usually quite different from one before 500. Provide all the information necessary to help your speaker. At this point you should also find out whether the speaker charges a fee.

Once you have obtained his or her consent to come, you should know how he will arrive (by car or plane, for instance) and where you will meet.

You may need to arrange for transportation and for overnight accommodations. If he or she prefers to get to the location on his own, he needs to know exactly where to go and how to get there.

Give your speaker a telephone number he can call at the last minute in case of emergency, and also the telephone number of the place where you will be meeting. And make sure that *you* know where your speaker may be contacted in case the emergency is at your end. Much can go wrong at the last minute, and it is important that the program chair or club president maintain a sure line of communication.

If you wish, and the speaker agrees, you might arrange a fifteen-minute informal coffee before the speech; some speakers like to get a feel for the audience before speaking. If the program chairperson plans a reception in the speaker's honor after the speech, you should also tell him that well in advance, and get his agreement. That also goes for interviews with the news media.

Once the speaker arrives, remember that he or she is your guest and should be treated as courteously as any stranger invited to your home. Either you or someone you assign must meet him at the door and then introduce him to people and make sure he is never left alone to fend for himself. Your most gregarious member may be the best person for this job.

Mealtime before a program may be agony for people who sit with the stranger they are going to hear; even presidents who are at ease and extroverted with their members can become tongue-tied and uncomfortable with a stranger. The stranger may feel shy, too. Just as in meeting anyone else, try to find common ground. Try talking about hobbies, or the problems of speaking and meeting with so many organizations. Does the speaker have a favorite city, a favorite vacation, a favorite lunch or dinner menu? Feel free to ask questions about the speaker's topic and express your own opinion, but don't be argumentative and don't be phony about your knowledge. You can be informative about your organization and help the speaker relax by letting him get to know you. Your guest will appreciate your warmth and friendliness.

As the program time approaches, your speaker probably will prefer not to talk. He needs time to organize his thoughts, prepare his opening remarks (perhaps based on what he has just learned from you and your group in the last minutes) and to compose himself. Therefore, fall silent. He'll chat if he feels like it.

Another courtesy you should offer your speaker is to *eliminate club business before the speech*. Few guest speakers enjoy sitting through your treasurer's report. Put club business after the speech so the speaker can gracefully escape. Some may wish to stay because they are interested or because they like to get a little feedback, but they should have a chance to leave if they wish.

Groups who meet at lunchtime may believe they are an exception to that advice, but I've learned that speakers feel just as strongly about being able to get away at lunchtime as they do at any other time.

A common discourtesy is the sloppy introduction. While the speaker spends much time preparing for an appearance, the introducer often spends no time at all learning about the speaker. It is deflating and disconcerting to speak without the sure knowledge that the audience knows enough about the speaker to establish his or her credentials.

As soon as your speaker agrees to come, ask him or her for a career résumé so that the introducer has time to prepare. If your speaker fails to send one, capture him before the program and ask for detailed information. Remind the introducer that an eloquent introduction is less important than an *accurate* and *complete* one.

Do not, for example, introduce a former legislator merely by giving her present title, Mrs. Jean Murphy, president of XYZ Carpenters, Inc. Do not introduce Frank Taylor as "president of the outdoor club" if he is actually chairman of the United Sportsman's Association. And list his credentials. He achieved his position by working on a number of important activities; name them. Finally, make sure the introduction fits not only the speaker but also the topic he will cover.

An exception could be when your guest speaks not as an individual but as a spokesperson for a company. In this case a detailed introduction is less important. His full title and any pertinent credentials may be enough. Then, make sure the audience knows something about the company he represents, such as "the Wheeler-Forman Company, maker of auto parts and located in Harperville."

Another common error is the statement, "I'm sure you are going to enjoy tonight's speaker." Somehow the word "sure" sounds too unsure. Instead, say, "I know we are all going to enjoy Ms. Smith's talk," and you have made a much more positive statement. If the speaker is dull, the audience will hold the speaker, not you, responsible.

Sometimes the person who makes the introduction decides that this is the time to make his own speech. He feels some personal comments are in order. They are not. To insert one's own personal biases or to take the speaker's time is rude. If you are the introducer, resist the temptation. If you choose the introducer, try to choose one who has good sense.

If you plan to present an honorarium, tell your speaker ahead of time what it is. Many speakers don't expect a fee, but if you can, set up a fund for a specific honorarium per speaker, depending on the size and influence of your group. (Thirty-five dollars to a local speaker is a good minimum target for the average organization of 100 members.)

I remember a snowy night when a small study group of farm women asked me to accept five dollars which they had decided should be their regular honorarium. Another year a church group dropped off a warm note of thanks and a gift at my door. When larger honorariums are out of the question, such actions go far to express a group's appreciation.

The homemaker who is a popular speaker may be

especially grateful for an honorarium; it will help pay for the extra clothes, personal care, baby-sitting and car expenses that are often part of speaking engagements. It also helps to resolve any guilty feelings that speaking engagements are a drain on the family purse. I know a delightful woman who was so eager to get her message across that she willingly spent her own money to fly to another state to speak. Not many people have that kind of dedication, nor can they afford it.

Today, more and more speakers realize that it is prudent, if only because people tend to appreciate something they have to pay for, to charge a fee, so don't be surprised to learn that a fee is expected. (A speaker of note, of course, will probably charge a hefty fee.)

Speakers coming from a distance will rightly expect reimbursement for travel expenses. Check with your business members or friends if you don't know the going rate for travel mileage.

The exception is the speaker who comes as a representative of a company, or who speaks during working hours as an employee of a public agency. The employee will tell you if the agency can't cover travel expenses.

There are proper ways to give your speaker the honorarium. If it is sizable, it may be mailed. Otherwise, give it gracefully and unobtrusively. A public display of counting out dollars into the palm of the hapless speaker—or just a flourish of money—is embarrassing. Instead, after the speech or meeting, give the honorarium in an envelope with as little fanfare as possible. Tell him or her what you are handing, because a keyed-up or distracted speaker may not pay attention to what he is receiving. All you have to say is something like, "This is your check, and we again thank you for coming."

### Planning for the Talk. How Much Time?

In this day of television, people are used to concentrating for only short periods of time. Therefore, a speech of twenty minutes to a half hour, followed by questions and answers, may be the most successful.

If you do allow questions and answers after your program, the program chairperson and speaker should agree ahead of time on how questions will be handled. That is, will the chair preside and repeat the questions, or will the speaker himself receive the questions? If the audience and the hall are large, and questions come from the floor, you will need to provide three or four floor microphones that the questioners can use. Some speakers prefer that questions be written out and passed up to the head table or podium. This avoids the need for microphones in the audience. The program chairperson should accommodate the speaker in those matters whenever possible.

### The Multi-Speaker Program

Special care must be taken when several speakers participate in the same program. A multi-speaker program presents multi-opportunities for disaster. You must plan a careful time sequence and give each speaker a definite, limited time. You will need tact, firmness and good sense. Unless your program is for an audience of assured size, or has special prestige, never ask more than one speaker to come some distance. Always be honest with your speakers when you invite them to speak; let them know exactly what is expected. The chair who invites ten individuals from across the state to participate in a two-hour program, and then lets them know after they arrive that they have only ten minutes to speak, is making certain that both his own and his organization's reputation will suffer.

Make it clear to your speakers—in writing—ahead of time how much time they will have to speak. Allow five to ten minutes between speakers for mistakes in timing, introductions, setting up slides, focusing the projector, etc Understand there may be problems you simply cannot foresee.

I will never forget the speaker who started to show

slides and discovered he had brought the wrong ones, then began to show lantern slides and discovered that they were too light to be seen, and then started on a prepared speech and discovered that all the pages were stapled out of order! By the time he gave up and spoke extemporaneously, the program schedule was a disaster.

At the beginning of your program, whoever is in charge should express great gratitude to the speakers for their presence, and remind everyone of the schedule. Then announce that, to be fair to all speakers, you have appointed Ms. Jones to keep everyone on schedule. Please forgive her, you say, but she will raise her hand before the last two minutes are up (or will stand, flash a light, wave, or dance a jig). Then Ms. Jones *must do it*. She must also have a different reminder when the speaker's time runs out. Your speakers were told in advance how much time they would have, so they won't be surprised or insulted by the (preferably unobtrusive) steps you must take to keep things on schedule. If the speaker keeps going beyond a few more words, the chair then steps up and gently takes over.

When you must use this procedure, you must implement it carefully. I was once given fifteen minutes to speak, but I was the last speaker. When my turn came, everyone else had used up my time. I had expended a good deal of effort preparing the talk and had driven 200 miles, yet finishing on time was evidently so important that I had barely started when the chairman began pointing to his watch and acting harried. On the other hand, I remember with chagrin and sadness that I was responsible for the same kind of thing happening to others. I had asked other people to chair the meeting and act as a monitor, and I sat buried out in the audience. Unfortunately, I had done a bad job of choosing my monitor. Despite his promise to be strict, one speaker went far beyond his allotted time. It destroyed all the planning.

The person who takes responsibility for a program must be sure he delegates responsibility to people he knows will do a good job, and he had better have a contingency plan if the first plan fails.

### The Panel Discussion

The panel discussion differs from the usual multiple-speaker program in both format and problems. Sometimes the panel is made up of two or three members of the club plus the outside guest speaker; another variation is that all the panelists are outside guest speakers who spoke earlier in the day. The program chair may introduce the panel chair, who then introduces the other members of the panel, or a moderator may introduce all the panel members. They then respond to questions from a moderator, or discuss among themselves questions given them from members of the audience.

Because so many variations are possible, your guest panelists should not be left to play it by ear. You (or the president, program chair, moderator, or whoever is in charge) should decide what format you are going to use, and then give the panelists specific written instructions well in advance of the occasion. Otherwise, you must sit down at least an hour before the program so that you and the panel members (including the moderator) can decide how to work it out. All hands should agree on procedure.

Try not to invite a panelist who dominates a discussion and takes far more than his share of time. If you end up with a talker, however, a strong moderator can control the situation. I have a gentle friend, much in demand as a speaker, who says that when he is a panel victim, he doesn't get upset; he just uses the time "to take a little nap." His complacency is admirable, but not shared by most busy people. You may avoid this and other problems if you rein in your enthusiasm and don't invite too many prominent people to participate. Certainly, the larger the size of the panel and the more prominent the panelists, the more you should know about panels and the more important is your selection of a moderator.

You should also remember that prominent people usually feel too busy to share time with other prominent people. You may invite key persons to participate, and they may accept. But once they learn how their time will be shared, they are likely to send a lesser light to take their place, and you may end up with a disappointed audience.

As in all cases, respect other people's time, and don't get inflated ideas about how your organization will use it.

### Subject Matter for Your Programs

Young people today seem to be obsessed by the concept of "relevance." Although they haven't always had enough experience to know what is relevant, they nevertheless make an important point. I've often wished that adults would be so obsessed.

In any organization, members should understand what their goals are and work within those goals. Otherwise, meetings merely clutter up our lives. It is appropriate for the social club, which exists simply to give its members a smattering of information and pleasure, to invite anyone from the latest celebrity to a visiting head-hunter to be its speaker. But parent-teacher groups, for example, should pay attention to what their purpose is: the cooperation of parents and teachers in the education and well-being of their children. It is appropriate and important for the PTA to offer programs dealing with such topics as how to help children study, getting to know the teachers, a school tax or school board campaign, and social and environmental problems that affect the lives of children. But programs such as cake decorating, fashion shows, or review of light-weight books are a waste of time for organizations with a purpose. The argument that these meetings bring out people and help them meet each other is specious.

That doesn't mean that play for play's sake should never be part of a year's program, but for the most part there's no reason that an organization can't plan programs that are both relevant and successful.

### *Physical Arrangements; Attending to the Details*

You will check ahead of time with your speaker to find out what equipment he or she needs, such as a slide projector or movie equipment. You should also ask if he prefers a particular height for a lectern. This seemingly small detail is important to a short person who must peer over a too-high lectern, or for someone who is near- or far-sighted, whose notes may lie too close or too far away to be read.

Once you find out your needs, the person in charge of these details must contact the meeting place in advance to make sure that all your requirements are met. Be sure to ask about extra charges. Some establishments have a practice of charging extra for such requirements as microphones, and the charge can be considerable.

A last-minute check the day of the meeting, well before people begin to arrive, is vital. Someone must be assigned to check, double- and triple-check the physical arrangement of the room and all the mechanical requirements. Make a checklist. What did the speaker say he needed? Do you have a podium of the right height? If it would help for the head table to be raised on a platform, ask whether one is available.

When it comes to projection equipment, assume it won't work. Never fail to have a dry run. That will at least save you from an embarassing, frantic search for an extension cord.

Be sure to remember a glass of water for the speaker. But don't make it ice water; that constricts the throat.

Some groups think that they must worry about details only if they bring a major speaker. (Then there are other groups who never worry!) No matter whether your speaker lives ten minutes or 1000 miles away, care enough about your speaker and audience to do everything possible to make your program go smoothly and comfortably.

### *Frustrations, Distractions, and Noise*

Though most members will never know firsthand the

frustrations that popular speakers constantly deal with, most people have had a familiar frustrating and miserable experience as part of an audience: a meeting in a hot or cold gymnasium-type room; hard folding seats scattered across the room; business conducted at a table without benefit of microphones and no one rising to speak; people at the back of the room neither seeing nor hearing; everyone else straining to hear or see.

I can't overemphasize the importance of thinking ahead of time about potential problems, including the difficulties the audience may have hearing and seeing. If, despite your best efforts, you end up in a room where almost nobody can hear or see, eliminate all but the most essential business. Don't let false modesty keep you or your other leaders seated when you should stand. Shout if you can't be heard. If one of your members came prepared to make a special report, apologize and explain why it's necessary to postpone it until the next meeting. Whenever unexpected difficulties arise, always be flexible and skip the nonessentials.

Distractions and noise can also ruin a good program. Again, do everything possible to avoid them. Both members and speakers will be driven crazy if the Goodworks Church auxiliary allows children to run around while someone is trying to talk. Any organization can figure out a solution to the problem of child care, and it is inexcusable not to do so.

Meetings in newer motels may mean loud music coming over a loudspeaker or from another room. Find out in advance if there may be this kind of interference, and go someplace else if they can't assure you that they will control noise. If noise becomes an unexpected problem, do your best to muddle through. Everyone will be annoyed, but unavoidable or unexpected disasters do happen. One Chamber of Commerce leader I know called a meeting of executives from around his state. The meeting was held in the plush board room of a bank. No sooner had the meeting begun, however, than electricians for another company on a floor below started drilling through a cement wall. Despite entreaties, the electricians wouldn't quit. Be assured that it isn't only "little" people in less prestigious organizations who die a thousand deaths when their best-laid plans go awry.

### The Right-Sized Room

An important psychological key to a successful program is to put your meeting in the right-sized room—the smallest space necessary to fit your audience comfortably.

A large room full of many scattered empty seats (with lots of empty seats right up front) is disconcerting to the speaker, puts the program chairperson into a deep fit of depression, and makes the organization feel less than successful. The better the room fits the number of people present, the more successful a program will appear. Fifty people in a large hall will look like a disaster; fifty people filling up a small room will look very successful indeed. One rule is to expect fewer people than you hope will come— because, unfortunately, those expectations will usually be right. If you simply have no way of knowing how many people may show up, arrange for a larger room than you may need, but set out a limited number of chairs at one end of the room, with extra folding chairs available. Let the arrangement look well planned by setting up some of the open area to serve coffee. It will be a psychological plus to have to pull out the extra seats. You may also be able to find a location in which the room can be made smaller by a folding door.

If you must meet in a large room with stationary seats, such as a church, you can cordon off the back half of the room so that people will be forced to sit up front and closer together in the area, which clearly says, "This meeting isn't a bust; we planned on this number."

### The Last Minute Effort

Once you have planned and done everything you can to insure a successful program, it helps to have a previously appointed committee call members. Since attendance is voluntary in most groups, a good turnout is more certain if a committee reminds members and gets them on the ball. Most of us need an extra push; it is so much easier to stay home or pursue other interests. Be kind to your organization and to your speaker by providing that last-minute effort to get people there. Everyone will appreciate the result.

**SUMMARY: Questions and checklist to guide you to a successful year's programs**

1. Are your proposed programs relevant to the purposes of your organization?

2. Are the programs varied from meeting to meeting? Should they be?

3. Do your proposed speakers have a reputation for giving good programs? Have you checked with people who have actually heard them?

4. Will you limit slide programs to thirty minutes for any but the most entertaining programs? Are you willing to limit the very best amateur programs to forty-five minutes? (When it comes to showing slides, many people simply have no sense.)

5. Do any of your programs allow your members to participate, such as through question periods, four-slides-per-member programs, and the opportunity to give advice regarding the type of programs they would like to have?

6. Will you and your organization be willing to prepare for and promote your programs effectively, so that your audience will be worth your speakers' time and effort?

7. Has everyone assigned to a job read this chapter carefully, so you avoid most of the mistakes most organizations make?

## Checklist

**ASSIGNMENTS TO BE MADE** (where relevant):

Program chair
Publicity chair
Tickets

Committee to call people to remind them to come

Hosts

Person to introduce speaker

Person responsible for honorarium

Person to write thank you letters

(Program chair is responsible for assigning someone to each of the matters listed below)

**SPEAKER** (All arrangements should be checked with and agreed upon by the speaker):

Length of time the speaker will have to speak

Subject of the program or speech; title for the speech

Format (speech and questions; panel discussion; movie; other)

Time of meeting; time of program

Location for meeting (exact room and directions given)

Time and place to meet speaker (airport, motel, meeting place; other)

Telephone numbers; contingency plans

Arrangements for hosting speaker throughout his or her visit

Transportation plans

Mealtime arrangements

Overnight accommodations

Honorarium or fee

Special plans ahead or after the program (cocktail party; tour; other)

Meeting with the news media before or after program

**EQUIPMENT NEEDS** (Also check with the speaker):

Slide projector

Movie projector

Screen or screens

Microphone(s)

Podium (how high?)

Other sound equipment; any other equipment needed

**MEETING PLACE** (Coordinate with equipment needs. Find meeting place and check arrangements well ahead of time. Don't forget possible need for posting signs—inside and out—and get necessary permissions.)

Room; check out size desired

Refreshments; meal (Time carefully; check out program and serving times)

Seats—number and arrangement

Tables for guests and equipment

Head table (placement of); decisions (written plan) regarding where each person at the head table will sit. Don't forget spouses of your VIPs.

Platform for head table (if necessary)

Table and table placement for ticket-takers, name tags, etc.

Chairs for the table

Problems: Check out regarding noise, other meetings, etc.

**LAST MINUTE PREPARATION** (So that you are ready at least an hour ahead of time):

All above matters, rechecked

Directional signs posted

All equipment checked for workability, proper placement

Podium checked for height

Glass of water for speaker

# Managing
# One's Life

**A**CTIVE VOLUNTEERS COME in both sexes and in all sizes, shapes, colors, and personalities. One thing they have in common: They feel guilty about the tremendous amount of time they put into their volunteer activities, and are dismayed over the many personal sacrifices they continually make.

Yet an active volunteer broadens the interests of the rest of the household by bringing them into contact with ideas outside home and business. Children learn from their concerned and active parents that there are needs to be served and responsibilities to be met beyond their own self-centered worlds. Volunteerism is an active example of willingness to cooperate and help others—and when deemed necessary, to change the world to make it a better place in which to live.

Nevertheless, volunteer work does put an extra stress on the home. Even without the responsibility of a family, a volunteer can find life overwhelming, with no time to meet ordinary responsibilities to friends and relatives. Every minute spent working without pay for another cause is a minute taken from one's own personal needs. The successful volunteer has to find ways to make the personal pluses outweigh the minuses. One way is to learn how to manage your life.

Like so many ideas in this book, this lesson comes from my experience. During much of my voluntary activism, it had never occurred to me that I could really control my life. All of my family, including me, suffered from my ignorance. It finally took a friend's example to teach me what I had long needed to learn.

A group of us in an active, growing organization decided that we simply had to have one paid person to run the show. Everyone was worn out and overcommitted; none of us could continue to be available regularly to oversee the immense amount of work that needed to be done. We raised just enough money to hire a part-time director, and went to a charming, hard-working volunteer to see if she would take the job. She said yes—with conditions. Because the job paid very little and her family was young, she insisted that a rule must be that nobody call her at night and that she should not be expected to work most nights or any weekends. We needed her, and we accepted her conditions.

I finally realized that I could do the same thing: decide how much time I was willing to give, and make rules for myself to help control my own life. Any volunteer can make the same kind of realistic agreement with the world. After all, nobody *makes* a volunteer do anything, even though really active volunteers *behave* as if everyone else in the world has a right to their time. It is important that volunteers take another look and decide how much of themselves they will give, and *when they will give it*.

Here are examples:

An attorney with special talents serves in extra capacities which require great amounts of unpaid time during the business day. To fulfill obligations to clients and firm, this person works long hours at night and some weekends. However, the attorney is totally *un*available to the outside world most weekends. Time is then reserved for self, children and spouse.

A busy homemaker, president of an active organization, has no preschoolers at home, so decides to be available for calls until 3:30 P.M. when the children arrive, and on weekday evenings after 8 P.M.

A doctor who cannot be available during the day—even to speak on the telephone—gives up two full evenings a week for volunteer work.

An unmarried teacher attends meetings and does extra work on weekends. Weekday evenings are reserved for personal pursuits.

In other words, your lifestyle and the type of volunteer job you accept should determine how much time you must give to do a good job, and when you will do it. It's up to you to decide how to put it all together.

### Controlling the Telephone

The telephone is the biggest problem to most active volunteers. It intrudes into business and the home, uninvited, at all hours of the day. There is no way to avoid this problem entirely, but with firmness and tact it can be controlled.

Unless you get a handle on the problem of the telephone, you will remember with horror those times you neglected your own or your family's important needs when other people's needs seemed to take priority. Remember that although the outsider's demands by phone may be uncontrollable, your *response* to those demands *is* controllable. You have every right to say, pleasantly and reasonably, "I'm happy to hear from you, Frank, but I can't talk now. Will you be free sometime during the day tomorrow?"

The volunteer who works and isn't available to talk during the day, and who has a family or lives with other people, has the hardest time working out a realistic plan for taking calls. However you schedule them, try to avoid talking on the phone near other members of your household. If you can, put a phone in another part of the house, and arrange to do your telephone business there.

If the phone becomes an instrument of torture in your household, and if you can possibly afford to put in another phone, consider getting another line (at the lowest rates) for your incoming organizational calls, so you can handle them differently from calls on the household line. Give out the second number just for organizational business. If that won't work, give the new, unlisted number to family and good friends so that, when desired, the ring of the listed phone can be ignored. (You might even list the "unlisted" number under an agreed-upon name that only close friends and family know. In case they lose the "unlisted" number, they can still look it up.)

One of the problems with the telephone is the unfortunate fact that some people just like or need to talk, and the telephone offers an easy way to do it. Lonely people, or people with personality problems, are sometimes telephone addicts. If you are a kind and sympathetic soul, you may become an innocent victim of their problems. Take a firm grasp on yourself and reality, and learn how to handle the situation. Fit these people into your schedule when the rest of the household is away, or during the specific hours you decide to be available, and limit the time you take with them. An organization leader must be willing to listen objectively to legitimate complaints, but remember that the year you play a leadership role is tough enough without also trying to play psychologist to telephone addicts. If you wish, you can accept that role another year.

Furthermore, no one should think he is obliged to listen to gossip. Once people understand that you aren't at all interested in petty complaints, they will stop complaining to you. This takes tact and responsiveness at important times. Most gossip comes from people who are insecure; let them know how important they are to you, and that is *all* that is important. A cheerful, "Jack, I can't tell you enough how much we appreciate all your hard work; I know you think Tom isn't doing his share, but we'll just have to get along with the situation as best we can," will go a long way. Jack is hearing what he needs most to hear—that he is important, and he'll get the hint quickly that you won't take time to hear complaints about other people.

If you take on a big job, then you may have no choice

but to give up a huge chunk of your time to take calls and do the necessary work. "Giving up for the cause" will be necessary when that very special project demands an unusual commitment for a period of time. Tell your family (or if you have no family, tell yourself!) how important you think the project is, and that you want to commit yourself to it for this year (or three months, or whatever) of your life. Enlist their interest and support if you can. Tell them that you *know* it will mean that you may be less organized, and you will be less available for their needs.

Warning and explanation may not help the family enjoy the confusion and your absence any better, but it will help them understand and appreciate the situation more.

During this time, it is even more important to take the phone off the hook, or shut off the bell, before and during meals. If you are responsible for children at lunchtime, reserve enough time so they can relax and spill their tales of joy and woe to you. The few minutes after children come home from school in the afternoon is another important time to be reserved for them. Many children give up when they must compete with the telephone. If you want your children to grow up feeling as responsible and caring as you do, you must find ways to give them the love and attention they require.

During the most pressing time of duty, you might also decide what is best for your nervous system. For instance, my husband pointed out to me that if I would resist working on problems just before I went to bed, sleep would come much faster, last longer, and be more restful. (It's true.) Eventually, I learned not to take business calls after 9 P.M., or write reports, or read about problems before going to sleep.

The idea of controlling one's life will make most volunteers nervous, but it works. Once you get used to the idea that you don't *have* to be available to other people or outside problems at all times—that if people need you enough, they will call back or you can call them—you will find life much more peaceful.

Try to foresee problems that will come up—the exceptions which should be made. If you decide, for instance, that you simply aren't going to talk after 9 P.M., you should also anticipate exceptions. (I used to accept long-distance calls no matter what the hour; I didn't want to pay for returning the call!) If you use common sense, you will be successful in deciding what takes priority.

### The Volunteer at Home

This section is primarily for the volunteer at home— who doesn't have an outside job and is responsible for maintaining the home. Because *all* his or her time must be voluntarily managed, this person often has the greatest problem managing it.

A big problem in managing one's time is to take time to be neat. An active volunteer is likely to have much paperwork to do. Too often, the papers end up on the kitchen counters and dining-room table. To maintain such a mess, however, is simply unfair to your family. Just as you must be orderly in business, so you must also be orderly at home. You have to solve this problem. When you do, you will solve a lot of others—like being ready when unexpected company shows up, and feeling in control of your home.

There are two all-important steps to eliminate the problems of continual disorder: First, no matter what else you have on your mind, no matter what tempts you to do something else, take care of your household tasks first thing in the morning. Second, find a space in the house to call your own. Do everything you can to organize that space for your own use.

Here are some suggestions: Buy (new or used) a desk and files. Make a bookcase out of bricks and boards. Put these together, and you have a good working area. Or, make two bookcases at table level and lay boards across the top of them to make a desk. A low filing cabinet can be used instead of one of the bookcases. Paint or wood-finish your boards and bookcases to go with your room, and you have a working area on which you can pile your papers neatly and efficiently.

If at all possible, put a telephone in your working area. Remember, however, that if it is your only telephone, it will be inconveniently placed if it interferes with you or others in your household. You might also want to put an extra-long extension cord on your phone. (This is great for moving around and getting other work done while you talk.) If you can't afford metal files, make use of cardboard files or even the paper accordion files you can buy in stationery and notion departments. Files help keep you organized.

If you hurt for both space and money, a card table with a makeshift bookshelf underneath will do. When you work, you can pull over a table or chairs so you can spread out your material. However you do it, create some kind of working arrangement so that the work can be piled up neatly afterward. And "afterward" means *before* your spouse comes home, or the rest of the family needs the space.

If your work is so immense that you must stack mountains of material, you may have to look for a place in the basement or elsewhere. What counts is that you recognize how easy it is to create a constant mess with volunteer work, and that somehow you must make arrangements so your activities don't interfere with the rest of the household.

### The Volunteer at Business

Businesspeople who do some of their volunteer work at the office have other problems. Although some companies* encourage community participation by their employees and by policy allow some of it to be done on company time, much volunteer work in the office must be fit in when the employee has (or takes) the time. The question of how much volunteer work an employee can legitimately do on the job can be a difficult one for the employee, and it can lead to trouble if the time isn't managed properly.

* I use the word "company" in the broadest sense. You may substitute institution, school, or whatever fits your place of employment.

Each job situation is different and I won't try to get into the special problems that depend on whether or not you are self-employed, whether your job precludes interruptions, whether your union makes special arrangements for attending meetings, whether you have a secretary, or even whether you have a telephone available.

You can't have a secretarial problem if you have no secretary; you can't decide about telephone interruptions if you can't be reached by telephone; and you don't have the worry of how to fit your volunteer life in with your business life if the problem is precluded by the type of job you have. If you are self-employed, most of the decisions on how much time you can, or are willing to, afford for volunteer work will be yours alone to make.

Of overriding importance is the question of how much volunteer work you can reasonably do during working hours. Even in a supportive company, such work can get out of hand if you aren't careful. A volunteer project may seem so important, or so exhilarating, or demands put on you by the outside world (telephone calls, letters, etc.) so insistent, that you get swept up into the activity. Soon you neglect your primary responsibilities to the people who pay you. Just as the person in charge of the household has to examine how well he or she is living up to primary responsibilities, so must you make a conscious decision about the time you devote to the outside project.

Examine what you are doing. Are your volunteer telephone conversations taking up large chunks of business time? Are you letting business slide? Are your co-workers having to do more work because of your volunteer efforts? Look carefully at what you are doing from the perspective of your boss, fellow workers and any employees under you, and make sure your work isn't adversely affecting them.

Your volunteer work can't be excused if you aren't fair to a secretary, or to anyone else who works with you. You should *never* give your volunteer problems to someone under you unless you are sure that your boss or company won't disapprove *and* that the employee can get his or her own work done without being too rushed or having to work over-time. Also, never ask someone else to help if the project violates his or her own personal feelings or beliefs. You wouldn't ask someone opposed to hunting to work on a hunting brochure, nor would you ask an anti-abortionist to help you with pro-abortion material. Feelings of others may not be strong: they may simply be uncomfortable about participating in your project. You must be sensitive to the perceptions of people with whom you work.

If people whom you involve at work have no particular interest in or knowledge about your subject, give them as much explanation as possible so that they participate more enthusiastically. This is important in any work you give other individuals; it is *vital* if that work isn't part of the job they believe they were hired to do.

Even if other workers aren't affected by what you do, it may be well to explain your activities to them to encourage their moral support. Years ago I was a young office aide, and I remember well how the secretaries were appalled at the company time an employee used for non-company business. His status in the company and the project he was involved in made his activities fully legitimate from the company's point of view, but the secretaries didn't know that, and on general principle it made them angry.

When you have the cooperation of your boss and any affected workers, you may find it most productive to do volunteer work at the office during office hours and make up the time evenings or weekends. That is how most business-volunteers manage their job and volunteer work successfully. Time can also be made up by not taking coffee breaks and shortening your lunch hour, letting others know that the time saved is being used for your volunteer calls and letter-writing.

In all cases, be honest with yourself about how the volunteer job is affecting your paying job. One way is to keep a careful record of exactly how much time you spend on the phone, dictating or typing letters, and attending meetings. The time may surprise and dismay you, and help you realize that you have to work out a different arrangement.

On the other hand, you may well be proud and glad for the time you spend, knowing that you are being fair to those around you and to those who employ you, and that you are also contributing greatly to the needs of the larger community. You willingly sacrifice the time (and salary if you are self-employed). This world is a better place to live because many others have also sacrificed their time and money.

When such decisions are made wisely, you can not only be a productive and significant employee; you, like the household manager, can also be a productive and significant member of the larger community of humankind.

### Setting Priorities

All volunteers find that a real burden is the demand to do too many little things: attend meetings, sell tickets, bring cookies, solicit funds, etc., etc. There are also spur-of-the-moment things you want to do for neighbors, friends and relatives. You must take stock of your activities, your job, and your family, and decide your priorities.

If you have children, their ages should help determine what your volunteer priorities are. If your children are very young, for instance, it is important to do your part for them in the school and community. Children have a much stronger sense of being loved, and a greater sense of security, if they know their parents are taking their turns in being responsible—whether it is in sending cookies for the class party, being a homeroom or den parent, an Indian-guide father, or whatever ordinary needs your schools, church or community have for parents' participation.

Children feel guilty when they sense they are a burden to other parents when their own parents could be available. Your first responsibility is to the children you are raising. Develop your priorities with your children in mind, but don't let them be your all-consuming priority. As they grow older, you should be able to give more time to adult responsibilities. The school board needs your interest and concern. The city commission needs active citizens paying attention to how the commission is fulfilling its responsibilities.

You can become educated by being involved. The average American occupation of sitting around the living room with friends, pooling their ignorance about the problems of the world, won't help solve those problems. Just as "not to decide, is to decide," so not to be involved is to be part of the problem.

To sum up, it is good to be involved, but it is also good to be wise about your activities. Decide how important a project is to you, your family, your job and your community. Decide what part you can reasonably play. Don't hesitate to turn down a plea if you feel that justice to your other responsibilities tells you that "no" is the best answer. Look at your whole range of interests. Remember that you can do a lot more if you are organized.

The old saw, "If you need something done, ask a busy person," is actually bad advice. The sooner leaders resist the temptation to ask a busy person and start asking less active people to do things, the sooner everyone will be better off. If you have accepted major responsibilities, *don't* accept minor duties unless it is to do something to show one of your children your personal support. Let others bring cookies for church functions, solicit money for the Community Chest, and serve on telephone committees. Take your turn doing these jobs when your other responsibilities are finished. You can't and shouldn't try to do everything and be everything to all people.

The more you allow and encourage others to participate, the more other people will become part of the volunteer pool. You may be surprised to discover how many people haven't rolled up their sleeves only because they don't realize how much they are needed and wanted, or because it is always easier to stand apart from the organization than it is to wade in and volunteer. The best, most innovative workers may be those people who simply need to be asked. *Do* take on the job of making sure somebody asks them.

Although it is easy for the committed, energetic, caring person to get trapped into a merry-go-round that is a burden for everyone, life doesn't have to be that way. By carefully deciding priorities and making rules for yourself, you will be able to get done what you want to do most—and you'll live far more responsibly, happily and graciously doing it. You'll be an effective person.

# Part II:

# Effective Organization Business

# Wolfe's Rules
of Order

**P**ARLIAMENTARY LAW OR procedure is the set of rules by which most organizations conduct their business. It comes down to us from English common law and the rules of Parliament. Except where such rules are part of an official organization's legal code, they are "law" in name only. The rules were written to protect the rights of the minority. They also provide a method for the orderly, courteous conduct of business.

Parliamentary procedure has been used in America since colonial days, but has been modified many times to fit special circumstances. In 1876, Henry M. Robert simplified the rules of Parliament and the U.S. Congress and gave lesser organizations a version of parliamentary law that is still famous and useful today. *Robert's Rules of Order* (or something similar) are essential to the orderly conduct of the meetings of large organizations, especially political bodies. And although these rules are lengthy and complicated, members of large groups should be well versed in them.

In small, informal groups, however, I believe that such detailed rules are not only not essential, they can be counterproductive. Unfortunately, most clubs and societies state in their bylaws that business shall be conducted by *Robert's Rules of Order*. Although the bylaws may say that, *Robert's Rules* are complicated and awesome, and few members take the time to read them, let alone learn them.

Hence, while most groups think they are adhering to *Robert's Rules,* most of them are not.

It makes a big difference. Organizations whose members think they use the rules as their guide, yet don't learn the rules, ask for trouble. And they get it. Members get all tangled up because they haven't a basic understanding of the rules, or they get into a wrangle trying to decide what Robert said. I've observed more than one group waste time deciding how long you're allowed to "lay a matter on the table," and I've attended a class in parliamentary procedure in which the instructor gave a different version than that found in *Robert's Rules.*

When some members don't have time to learn all the rules, others with a superb grasp on them can easily take advantage. We've all heard of the parliamentarian lawmaker who uses the rules of Congress to his own end. This also happens in smaller groups.

A friend tells about serving as the student member of a prestigious adult board of directors. A member suddenly moved to close debate. "But . . . ," my friend started to say. The other members admonished him, saying (correctly, according to Robert) the motion was not debatable. If the student had known parliamentary law better, he would have known he could "rise to a point of order," and protest that he hadn't been given a chance to speak on the issue. (That's a basic parliamentary right of each member.)

Not knowing the rules—or not being quick enough to remember them—is such a real problem that parliamentary manuals warn their readers to study the rules carefully so as not to work under a severe handicap. The manuals point out that the rules weren't written to hinder business (quite the contrary), but that's what sometimes happens.

In truth, *Robert's Rules,* and most "simplified" parliamentary rule books, include many more rules than the small or informal group needs. For instance, a parliamentary handbook advises that a person bothered by noise may interrupt by saying, "I rise to a question of privilege," and use that rule to ask that the door be shut. In a large, formal group, raising a question of privilege is polite and shows others that you are using a proper procedure; you aren't just some nut calling out for attention.

In an informal setting, however, persons unfamiliar with the rules would think your action pompous. The person troubled by noise should simply say so; he doesn't need to "rise to a question of privilege," and he doesn't need to remember that rule.

Still another problem with *Robert's Rules* is that when some members stick strictly to them, the rules make a meeting dull or even absurd. That also happens in large organizations, but in my view the benefits there outweigh the problems.

I'm sure the writer of a parliamentary handbook didn't mean to be ridiculous when he gave the following example, but it illustrates an overemphasis on rules. The author explains that a "privileged motion" takes precedence over other motions, and that a motion to adjourn takes precedence over them all. His example is a faulty furnace causing a room to fill up with smoke so that members could hardly breathe. Obviously, according to the author, someone should move to adjourn, the motion be put to a vote, and if the majority agrees, the meeting should adjourn no matter what other business is before the group.

But if it would be "absurd," as the author also maintained, to stay in the room, then it would be absurd to take time for a motion and vote.

The author would have seemed far less autocratic, and the rules far less overwhelming, if he'd used that example to explain the proper way to use the phrase, "If there is no objection (we are adjourned)." Or better yet, the author could have omitted that example altogether, depending on the common sense of the chair to handle the situation.

A happy solution to all the preceding problems would be for everyone to learn *Robert's Rules of Order,* believe in them, and use them with skill and common sense. But that hasn't happened and it's not going to happen. Since the complete rules aren't necessary in most groups anyway, the practical solution is to follow simple rules, and not call them *Robert's Rules*. That way, no parliamentarian in the group can have an advantage, time won't be wasted trying to figure out what Robert says, and business can proceed with a minimum of formality and grief.

I serve on a policy-making body of a large agency. One of my fellow commission members, an attorney, warned us to avoid saying that we follow *Robert's Rules*. We took his advice, and omitted such reference in our Administrative Rules. Although we may sound less impressive and we do get muddled sometimes, we don't get bogged down in parliamentary procedure, either. Our mistakes are made when someone isn't clear about what he or she wants, or when we forget very basic parliamentary procedure.

Because I am suggesting that informal organizations *not* follow *Robert's Rules*, a caveat is in order: *Robert's Rules of Order*, or a similar version of parliamentary law, and their explanations, are valuable to read, study and remember, even if you never use them. They will help you clarify in your own mind the logic of organizational procedure. They will help you be more effective. Certainly if you find yourself in a group where *Robert's Rules are* used, knowledge of them is essential to your effectiveness.

Group members should know basic procedure based on parliamentary law; they should follow *something*. You may want to use the following guidelines, or develop your own. Whatever you adopt, put them in writing and give them to your members. No matter what your rules, they won't always prevent confusion. A good chairperson is important for keeping things on track, and member logic is necessary. Although you will sometimes get muddled with simplified rules, you will waste no more time than if you try to follow more detailed ones, and everyone will be a lot more comfortable.

# Wolfe's Rules of Order

## GENERAL

### Responsibilities of the members

1. Always be courteous. Abusive behavior is out of order.
2. Speak after you have been recognized by the chair. (The chair may waive this rule in a very small group.)
3. Unless the group is sitting so that everyone can clearly see the faces of everyone else, stand when you speak.
4. Interrupt only for business that needs to be taken care of before the business presently on the floor. You may do this without first seeking recognition from the chair.

### Responsibilities of the chair

1. Keep order.
2. Protect the rights of all members.
3. Give everyone a chance to speak before calling on anyone a second time, except—at your discretion—the person who made the motion. The chair may add to the discussion after giving others a chance to speak, but do not argue strongly from position as a chairperson unless the group is so small that the chair also participates as a member.**
4. After one person speaks on one side of an issue, recognize someone else who will speak on the other side, if you know who stands on which side.
5. Allow only one issue on the floor at a time.
6. You may set limits to a debate so long as everyone has the chance to speak at least twice.**
7. You must entertain all motions (accept them for seconding and allow members to vote on them).

** This indicates throughout this section that *Robert's Rules* or other parliamentary books deal with the subject differently.

## MAIN MOTIONS

A main motion is a proposal to do something beyond incidental business, and becomes the main subject under discussion.

### *Two main motions are never discussed at the same time.*

A main motion which contains two separate ideas should be *divided* into two separate motions. This may be done at the time the original motion is made. The chair asks the person who made it to separate the issues and move only one of them at a time. If the motion isn't divided right away, it may be divided by amendment later.

### *Motions are expressed positively, never negatively.*

Motions are made to propose an action. Do not move *not* to do something.

### *Motions should be explicit.*

State fully what you want your motion to do. If you want to postpone an action, for instance, include when the matter can be brought up again: "I move that we postpone action on this matter until the committee looks at the alternatives and gives us a recommendation." Or just, "I move we postpone this matter until we have more information."

### *Motions that are long and complicated should be written.*

Hand the motion to the chair, who should read it and pass it to the secretary, who should take it down and hand it back to the chair.

### *Motions are handled in the following way:*

Somebody says, "I move that (the group do such and such)." The chair repeats the motion and asks if there is a second. Anyone may second it by saying, "Second," or "I second the motion."

### *Motions must be seconded, or they die without discussion.*

Seconding a motion does not necessarily denote agreement. A member may second a motion merely to give the motioner a chance to explain his motion. In that case, the seconder may want to preface his second with the remark, "For purposes of discussion, I second the motion."

*As soon as a motion is made and seconded, it is "on the floor" and discussion must be allowed.*

The form for the chair is, "The motion to (do such and such) has been made and seconded. Is there any discussion? Even if the motion came as a result of much previous discussion, the question must still be asked.

*Motions, once seconded, belong to everyone.*

The member who introduced the motion can't withdraw or change the motion without agreement from the group. The person who made the motion can interrupt discussion and *move* that it be withdrawn; or the chair, upon seeing that there seems to be agreement that the motion should be withdrawn, may ask the proposer if he or she wants the motion withdrawn. If the answer is yes, the chair should say, "If there are no objections (pause) the motion is withdrawn."

## AMENDMENTS

*Amendments are motions that change the main motion. They are made to:*

1. Add or insert new words
2. Take out words
3. Substitute one motion for another; and
4. Divide the motion so that separate subjects are dealt with separately.

*An amendment may even make the main motion mean the opposite of its original intent.*

If you had a motion on the floor to "increase the size of the sanctuary," somebody could move to amend the motion so that the word "increase" is changed to "decrease." If that amendment were passed, you would then be voting on a main motion totally different from the original proposal. (You have probably read about members of Congress who fight hard for a bill, and in the end vote against it. The reason is usually that the bill was amended [changed] so greatly that they could no longer support it.)

*Amendments are always voted on in reverse order, and no voting is done until all the amendments have been offered.*

Amendment number 3 is voted on before 2, which goes before 1. That's the only way to know what you're voting on. (See paragraph above.)

*The amendment process should be limited. Groups should never try to handle more than three amendments at a time.*

Too many amendments confuse members. When this happens, the chair should suggest that the motion and amendments be withdrawn, more discussion held, and the motion-making process started over. Often some of the amendments appear agreeable to everyone and could be part of the main motion. The chair can do this if there are no objections. If there are objections, or if the chair doesn't make the suggestion, a member may move that all the motions be withdrawn and that the group start over. This motion, if seconded, is voted on without debate.

## DISCUSSION AND DEBATE

The person who made the motion speaks first. All members must have a chance, if they wish, to speak at least twice on any issue. The chair may express his or her opinion.** The chair doesn't get into full debate, however, and usually speaks last. In committee, a committee chair participates as fully as any member. Debate continues as long as anyone has something new to say, or is limited or cut off by a 2/3 vote of the members.

## VOTING

When discussion is over, the procedure to vote is as follows: Chair says, "If there is no more discussion" (but if members voted to cut off debate and "move the previous question," however, the chair omits that phrase), "the vote is on the motion to . . . All those in favor of the motion say 'aye' (or 'yes')." The people agreeing with the motion vote aye, or yes, in chorus. Then the chair says, "All those opposed say 'nay' (or 'no'). Depending on the vote, the chair then announces, "The motion carries," or "The motion fails." If a voice vote is close, the chair will need to ask for a show of hands on each side of the issue. Where it is important to know how people voted (for board minutes, for example), the chair may call the roll, and each person votes when his name is called. In all cases the chair announces whether the motion carried or failed. He or she doesn't state how many for and how many against unless that is a question of importance to the group as a whole. Never call attention to the group's differences unless it serves a purpose.

Ordinarily the chair votes only to break a tie. However, in a meeting of the board of directors, the chair may vote to make a tie so that the issue can go to the entire membership for a vote.

In very small organizations, the membership may decide that it is important for the chair to vote as an ordinary member.

If the vote is an election, the voting should be done by ballot to insure secrecy.

## VOTE TO RECONSIDER

*Members may take up an issue as many times as they wish.***

A "motion to reconsider" can only be made by a person who voted for the proposal in the first place. The same person cannot make this motion more than once. Anyone can second it.

## OTHER TERMS AND EXPLANATIONS

### Close debate

This term means there may be no more discussion on the motion presently on the floor. To close debate when people are still discussing a motion requires a motion from a member. ("Moving the previous question" means the same thing.) The chair may cut off debate on an issue only if there is no motion on the floor.

1. A member is permitted to comment only once on this motion, and the comment must only be a statement on why the debate should not be closed.** It cannot be a comment on the motion that was being discussed.
2. To close debate requires a 2/3 vote to pass.

### Limit debate

1. The motion must include how the discussion will be limited (e.g., two minutes each, or only for those who may not yet have participated, etc.)
2. This motion is not debatable.
3. It requires a 2/3 vote to pass.
4. The Chair may rule to limit debate after a motion has been made and discussion begun.**

### Consensus

This is general agreement reached either immediately or after discussion. It may be agreement reached by compromise. After a lengthy discussion, and when consensus appears to have been reached, the chair may call for a motion—or, to save time—may state what appears to be the consensus of the group, and say, "*If I hear no objections* (always pause), we will do (such and such)."

### Unanimous consent

See last sentence, above, for an illustration of unanimous

consent. This device adopts an action as if the members voted on it. It is a useful, timesaving way to keep business moving when there appears to be agreement. It is best to use unanimous *consent* (as opposed to a unanimous *vote*) only for getting details out of the way quickly, and for moving business when it begins to get tangled.

### Consensus decision-making

This is a process of decision-making by general agreement rather than by vote. Some organizations use only consensus decision-making procedures when deciding on any major question. Action isn't taken unless a consensus forms.*

### Lay on the table

This is a much-used motion over which there is a lot of parliamentary confusion. Use it to postpone, but in your motion add, "until" (something happens, or another date.)** Always make motions as specific as possible.

*Legitimate interruptions: Use the form, "Excuse me, (Mr. or Madam) Chair, but . . . ** (Don't worry about using the specific phrases below.)*

Matters of *"privilege"* are personal matters that affect the group and should be taken care of before business goes on, such as getting a door shut so you can hear, or informing the chair that the organization's expert on the matter was called out of the room.

---

* Consensus decision-making, as an alternative to majority-vote procedures, empowers those holding minority opinions to block motions that are unacceptable to them. There are good reasons for its use in special situations, and it deserves some discussion. Consensus procedure has a long history in the American Friends Society. The League of Women Voters also makes its major decisions by consensus.

Decision-making by consensus is becoming increasingly popular with groups that wish to stress strong group cohesion. Consensus tends to heighten constructive criticism, encourage compromise, and avoid any tyranny of the majority. On the other hand, the process can be frustratingly slow. Even worse, in unfriendly situations, a group can find itself locked into the status quo by a minority of stub-

*Rising to a point of order:* You interrupt to point out that an error in procedure has been made and must be corrected before business proceeds. You may, for instance, need to point out that the group is discussing a new motion or subject when another motion is still on the floor. To get attention, you might prefer to call out, "point of order."

## Motion to adjourn

You may not interrupt for this motion, but once you make it, it takes precedence over all other motions except one to set the time and place for another meeting. In other words, other business can be stopped and this takes its place.

1. This motion is debatable.

2. It may be amended to fix the time and place for the next meeting.

3. Requires a 2/3 vote.

   (Note: If you are in a continuous session, for instance for several days, or if you simply want to break for meals, the proper word is *recess* when you break. You *adjourn* when the meeting session is completed and business is all over for the entire session.

## On the floor

Means that the subject has been moved and seconded, and is the topic of discussion and decision.

---

born naysayers who refuse to accept important proposed changes. Other groups require one or two meetings to try to reach consensus, and if they fail, only then resort to voting—and then they often require an 80–20 percent majority.

Consensus decision-making is still rapidly evolving. For new groups trying to decide which procedure to use, I would at this time recommend it only for small, creative groups whose members hold an unusual amount of good will toward each other. Whatever method is used, however, you should remember that the critical element in good group decision-making goes beyond the mechanics of procedure and consensus-versus-majority vote. Good group decisions depend on carefully listening to all viewpoints, gathering as much information as possible, and considering all ramifications of the choices.

### Open for debate

The subject has been moved and seconded and is ready to be debated.

### Out of order

A subject is "out of order" if it is discussed at the wrong time, that is, when something else precedes it on the agenda, or if another motion is already on the floor. If the chair doesn't stop the discussion and rule that the subject is out of order, a member may interrupt to point it out.

### Point of order

See discussion under legitimate interruptions.

### The question

This simply refers to the subject under consideration. "The motion on the floor is . . . Are you ready for the question?" (Here's the motion, are you ready to vote?) The chair never asks this until he or she first asks if there is any more discussion, or after debate has been closed by a 2/3 vote. When members call out "question," it should only mean they are *suggesting* that debate be closed. The chair should consider this only if everyone has made his points. The chair should not be intimidated by impatient or rude members if new information is still being brought forward. If a motion is on the floor and people still want to speak on it, debate can only be closed by a 2/3 vote by the members. (Or, as previously mentioned, the chairperson of a small group may rule to limit debate.)

### Quorum

Means the *number of members* that must be *present, or voting*, to enact business. Your organization bylaws should state what your quorum is. In most informal groups, a quorum is whoever shows up for a properly called general meeting. You may want more stringent requirements for the board of directors. The organization may also require a quorum of

2/3 of the membership present to vote on specific matters, like a change in the bylaws. A quorum is not the same as the percent or number of *votes* necessary to pass a motion. Usually this is a simple majority of the people voting (one over half the votes), except in special cases like the 2/3 vote needed to close debate.

### Received as read

This is the term to use for the treasurer's report and for any committee report that the group doesn't have time to examine fully at the time it is read. The chair says, "If there are no changes" (or after any changes have been made), the treasurer's report is "received as read" (or "received as corrected"). You wait until you have an auditor's report, and *that* is *approved.* The secretary's report is "approved as read," or "as corrected," because members can judge its accuracy at the time it is read. (To "adopt" or "accept" a report also means to approve it.)

### Stepping down from the chair

The chair may temporarily turn the gavel over to the vice-chair or person next in line, and that person chairs the meeting so the "former" chair may participate actively as a member. This method is also used when the chair prefers not to participate at all, such as when he or she has a conflict of interest. The chair only steps down to participate as a member if his feelings about a subject are strong, or if he feels he has information he must communicate in a less auspicious manner. The chair may step down without telling members why.

*To sum up*: "Wolfe's Rules of Order" are not original with me. Most of them come directly from *Robert's Rules* and general handbooks on parliamentary procedure, except that I have left out many details. I suggested modifying a few rules because I believe that the informal group is better served by not being so strict. (In those cases, I indicated a difference by the use of **.) Mainly, what I have tried to do is simplify parliamentary law so that informal groups use enough rules to help them move along, but no more. Nothing is set in concrete. Any group can make its own rules; perhaps you will find that my suggestions will give some guidance.

"Wolfe's Rules" assume a number of things: that the group is friendly and wants to stay friendly; that most members will not take the time to learn detailed parliamentary procedure; that your chairperson has good sense; and that the group is not so large or formal that it needs to be mandated by a detailed structure. Finally, because "Wolfe's Rules" were written to be remembered, and therefore don't cover all situations, they give the chair authority to arbitrate matters of procedure unless the members vote to overrule the chair.

These rules probably come close to the way most organizations already run their business. They are designed to clarify your procedure and make things easier so that everyone is on the same wavelength as you try to "do things right."

*Note*: A number of editions of *Robert's Rules of Order*, by General Henry M. Robert, are available in bookstores and libraries. Much of my information comes from *Parliamentary Practice: An Introduction to Parliamentary Law*, by Henry M. Robert (New York: The Century Company, 1921) and *Robert's Rules of Order*, again by Robert, (New York: Pyramid Communications, 1976) which includes a history by Floyd M. Riddick, former parliamentarian, U.S. Senate, and a commentary by Rachel Vixman. Explanations and simplified versions of parliamentary procedure are also available. Organizations such as unions, service clubs, and university extension services are among the sources for such information.

Particularly clear *Simplified Guidelines to Parliamentary Procedure* (subtitle) are found in *The Meeting Will Come to Order*, by Harold Sponberg, published by the Michigan State University Cooperative Extension Service, East Lansing, Michigan, 48824 ($.50). An explanation of complex parliamentary procedure, usefully organized, is *Parliamentary Procedure at a Glance*, by O. Garfield Jones (New York: Hawthorn Books, 1971). I also used those sources. Over the years I have used so many sources for the rules that I cannot remember or credit them all.

I should make clear that my suggested rules simplify parliamentary procedure beyond any other guidelines I have seen.

# Raising Money

S OME ORGANIZATIONS HAVE developed such rewarding fund-raising projects that continued success is assured. For them, raising money may be plenty of work, but no major problem. For others, however, no subject can seem more painful.

Raising money doesn't have to be such a discouraging proposition. It gets that way mainly because groups get into uninspired ruts. An organization generally assumes the ways and means chairperson will follow the group's old, tired routes for raising money, and so funds continue to be raised with reluctance and with difficulty.

Instead, appoint an enthusiastic (or at least determined) ways and means committee. Let it be composed of your most creative thinkers. Be sure that some of them are workers who will help follow through when final plans are made. Charge the committee with coming back to the board or membership with new ideas and recommendations. Ask them to develop immediate, easy plans if you need some funds quickly, but, if needed, also ask that they look into larger plans with the prospect of larger earnings. The best money-raising projects usually follow these guidelines:

1. The project takes as little time as possible for the most dollars raised, *or* is a project in which the service provided is more important than the profit per hour.

2. The project requires no large financial risk, *or* that risk can reasonably be borne by the group if the project fails.

3. The project is relevant to the aims of the organization, *or* the project makes so much money that relevance is unimportant.

4. The project helps publicize the organization and its purpose, *if* publicity is important to the group.

5. The project is fun and helps members get to know each other better, or the project is a service which gives members self-respect and an opportunity to be useful to others.

Your organization should decide on your financial goals so the ways and means committee knows how large a project they should be talking about. Groups often set a budget only after they figure out a project. It's a haphazard way to go about business. Do you need money or don't you? What are your priorities?

If you have a range of wants, then ask the committee to look into alternative projects based on different financial returns. The group as a whole can then be told: If we do project X, we hope to earn so many dollars, and we can do this and this. If you choose project Y, our return will be smaller, and we'll limit our spending to such and such activities.

If your group decides that its needs are modest, you may be able to raise the needed funds by telling members that they won't have to be bothered with a large fund-raising project if most members give a few dollars over the membership dues. Your committee might also suggest that you chuck the usual project and do something simple, such

*Note:* I hope in this chapter to give you only some general principles and a few ideas. An excellent source for more detail and information is *The Grass Roots Fundraising Book,* by Joan Flanagan, for The Youth Project, (Chicago: The Swallow Press, 1977). See also *Putting the Fun in Fundraising* by Phillip T. Drotning, (Chicago: Contemporary Books, 1979).

as throwing an informal party for the members and charging a small amount per person. Unless your members can't afford this kind of fund-raising, a cocktail party, spaghetti dinner, potluck or other simple membership affair might be the easiest and happiest solution to the annual problem of raising a modest amount of money.

Another simple fund-raiser within your group is the "silent auction." Members donate items (white elephants, used books, or anything else) and people bid by slipping their offers under the articles. Or the ordinary white elephant sale or book sale among members can substitute for the silent auction; let the members set the prices on their own donations.

If your money needs are more extensive, then the committee should consider projects which help express the purpose of your organization. The committee can examine your goals and try to find a project that enhances not only your purse, but also your reputation and your purpose.

Some organizations provide important community services, and your committee might examine whether your fund-raising project can be tied to a service. Senior citizens, for instance, can provide badly needed baby-sitting, tutoring or job-skill services and share some of the profit with the organization. Hospital auxiliaries have traditionally provided services to hospitals and their profits have largely gone to provide still more services. Other groups could be as useful. What kinds of service needs are unmet in your community? A little thought and research by the committee might uncover some exciting ideas.

Remember that whatever your project, you can add zest and interest to it. One group gave specially printed T-shirts to young people who raised a certain amount of money for them. Another awarded tiny plants (cost negligible) to people who brought items to their recycling center a given number of times; the group was astounded at how much more popular their center suddenly became.

The committee should go about its task in the mood to brainstorm ideas. Later, when the committee comes up with what it finally thinks is the best project(s), it should do a bit of homework before it brings its recommendation(s) to the membership.

The committee should learn whether any legal requirements stand in the way. Licenses or permits may be needed, and it is important to know whether these will be mere nuisances or real roadblocks.

The committee also needs to know whether any major costs are entailed. In the early stage of planning, ideas may not be well enough formed to acquire all the necessary information, but the more the committee learns, the fewer problems it will have describing the idea and eliciting support from the members.

Once your members enthusiastically endorse a project, the next step is deciding who will do what. This is crucial. You must have enough promises of time, energy and leadership to make the project a success. Otherwise, forget the idea and start over.

Then, the committee for the specific project must be formed. This may be the same ways and means committee, or it may be a new group, or a mixture of several of the original committee members and other willing club members. It's possible that someone who didn't serve on the ways and means committee is the most logical person to carry out the project. No problem here, so long as the ways and means chair and the special project chair agree upon and define individual responsibilities.

Once the project chairperson is appointed, the next step is to assign duties. The better the ways and means committee did its homework, the easier it will be to define duties and appoint the people to carry them out. The project committee chair will be responsible for the following:

*Planning.* Talk to others who have participated in similar projects. What problems can be foreseen? Where can help be found? Leave no stone unturned in learning as much as you can about what needs to be done. The ways and means committee should have done much of the groundwork, but there still may be much more to be learned.

*Preliminary arrangements.* Once you know your needs, people must be assigned to do the work. Preliminaries may be arranging for a program or speaker; identifying the time and arranging for the place; getting any required official permits.

*Publicity.* Even if the project is a simple sale among your own members, someone must be responsible for informing and gaining enthusiasm from the members. Many a member project is a dud because members aren't given enough information. If the project is larger and needs outside support, your publicity needs are much more extensive. (See the chapter on publicity.)

*Ticket sales.* If tickets are needed, who will get them printed? Who will keep track of the sales? Who will sell at the door?

*Finances.* Can the treasurer handle this project, or will you need someone else to help the treasurer?

*Service coordination.* If your project is one in which members provide individual service in the community, someone has a heavy coordinating responsibility. You'll want that person to be capable, pleasant and extremely conscientious.

*Donation of articles.* This is often a hard job, requiring more than one volunteer. If new or valuable donations are sought, then it is good to have special cards printed as an official receipt. The card should provide space for writing in the donor's name, the item donated and its monetary worth, and a signature. When people outside the organization donate items, a thoughtful action is to assign people to call or write each donor after the event to tell him how things went, how his donation helped, and how much the project earned. It's more fun to give if recipients act as if they care.

*Final arrangements.* Someone must be assigned to make sure the necessary equipment and people are on hand. What equipment will you need? Do you need ushers or hosts? Have you included every detail possible, and are you keeping lists? How about a clean-up committee? (If you're bringing a speaker, see the chapter on programs.)

*Keeping a record.* Throughout the planning and after completion of the event, the chair should keep a record in a looseleaf notebook. The more detailed the record—about contacts, aids, trouble spots, costs, publicity and everything else involved—the better and easier your event next time around. Even if the project fails, what you learn is important. As soon after the event as possible, assemble the major workers and rehash the project. People will have ideas for next year, and valuable reminders to include in the notebook. Ask them to bring you a written list of everything they think is important, and add to that information after the group has a chance to discuss it.

Finally, remember that it is only when groups sell unwanted products, or engage in time-consuming, unrewarding projects, that raising money is truly burdensome. If your group is creative, plans well, and has fun while it earns, everyone will find that raising money is easier and more satisfying.

Raising money may never be your favorite activity. On the other hand, your group may surprise itself!

## *Some Money-Raising Ideas*

Many of the following ideas are popular projects for fundraising. Others are so difficult that they may seem far-fetched. It's up to your group to decide what is most appropriate. Remember that this list isn't complete; your committee may come up with a far better idea. The suggestions can also be varied, and I hope you do have new thoughts to make your project more interesting. A new wrinkle on an old idea is often the best plan of all.

**SALES:** The longer you plan and the more goods for sale, the more possibility for large earnings.

> Rummage
>
> Community auction
>
> Used books
>
> New books
>
> New articles
>
> Baked goods
>
> Articles your members make
>
> Raffle tickets

**SERVICES:** Some of these suggestions are badly-needed services for which many people cannot pay the going rate. If your group can provide these services at minimal charge, you will have a worthwhile purpose for being.

> Baby-sitting
>
> Daycare at a center
>
> Meals served
>
> Driver service
>
> Tutoring
>
> Services in hospital or other institutions
>
> Car washing

Pet-sitting or care (when the owner is away), or pet services (such as walking, bathing, etc.)

Odd-job work

## PASSIVE ENTERTAINMENT:

Popular programs, speakers, or entertainers

Demonstrations

Children's programs

A fair, carnival, or play put on by the members

A special theater or movie day

## OTHER EVENTS:

Efforts for which people pledge money

Selling in a store, on commission

Social occasion, for a donation

Games, such as bingo (Note: you'll need a state license; or this may not be legal in your state)

"Gambling" parties using fake money (Check with authorities)

Visits to historical or other special homes

# Elections

**E**LECTIONS ARE SUPPOSED to insure that an organization continues to have responsible and responsive leaders. Members expect their leaders to get things done, and action depends on the kind of leaders they elect. Unfortunately, the way many groups hold elections, the people most likely to be elected are the people least likely to effect progress or action. Let me explain.

Who are the most eager, enthusiastic members in most organizations? Generally, they are a combination of the newest members and a few solid, interested, hard-working older members. But the usual way of holding elections makes it difficult to bring into the leadership circle the new, eager group.

Why? Elections are ordinarily carried out after a nominating committee selects at least two persons to run for each office. If the group is large, a profile of each nominee is included with the ballots and sent to the members. Whether the organization is large or small, the multiple-slate election—rather than a single slate of nominees selected by the nominating committee—has serious built-in disadvantages:

1. It hurts a bit not to be elected by your fellow members. Unless there is some overwhelming reason why a multiple-slate election must take place, it seems unnecessary and counterproductive to hurt, even momentarily, people who volunteer their free time for a good cause. A horrible

example is when a nominating committee selects only one or two more nominees than are actually needed for, say, twelve or fourteen places on the board of directors. In one such case in my memory, the most creative, hardworking, popular woman in our local club was unknown at the state level and therefore was the one person not elected.

2. Often a nominating committee is hard put to find many truly active people who represent the concerns of the members. The committee takes its responsibilities seriously, talks to other members and the present board of directors, and tries to find the best workers and thinkers to give the board a good balance. But with more nominees listed than are actually needed, the final composition, or "balance" elected to the board will be accidental.

3. In a large organization, the members don't know all the individual nominees and don't know how effective they have been on various committees. They vote on the basis of the profile given them. Profiles can be extremely misleading. More than one election has produced board members who (1) have impressive sounding backgrounds and points of view, but who work poorly with other people, or (2) are so busy on other matters that they give little time to the group, or (3) have given so much time in the past that they no longer feel compelled or inspired to put out the needed effort. If the nominating committee had chosen only a single slate—one person to an office—it would not have had to fill out the slate with people who probably won't do the job. The committee would have felt more responsibility to make sure there were real workers on the board, and would have recognized that it is important to bring in new people. The multiple list of nominees therefore produces a preponderance of board members who are elected primarily because they are well-known or their profiles read well. The organization loses the opportunity to bring in the new, hard workers and creative thinkers.

(*Note:* There are two kinds of groups for which it may

make good sense to have multiple-slate elections: statewide and nationwide groups with an adequately large *full-time staff*. The board members are not needed for doing most of the work; they are elected to make sure that the chief concerns and viewpoints of the members are properly represented. Profiles are helpful to give members an idea of the backgrounds and viewpoints of the prospective leaders. Day-to-day action is not dependent on these people.)

The only reason for elections is to continue to have active, responsive leadership. Therefore, although at first glance a one-slate election may seem undemocratic, I believe it is the key to getting good leaders.

A couple of built-in protections make the one-slate system democratic. There should always be space provided on the ballot, or nominations opened up on the floor, so that there is an *opportunity* to elect other people. Further, the bylaws should limit the number of years anyone can serve as an officer or member of the board.

Also, in any democratic group the leaders will continue to keep in touch (by polls or other methods) with the opinions of their own members. If members are unhappy about the direction the group is taking, they have opportunities to express their dissatisfaction very effectively. That is, members can always put their money and efforts into one of many other similar organizations. Most groups are competing with others, so they don't get far off-base (for long) in representing their members.

Therefore, I encourage you to give your nominating committee clear guidelines to come up with a *single* slate of officers and board members. The committee, appointed by the president, should be composed of three or five members chosen because they are interested in the goals of the organization but are ineligible or not interested in an office that year. Nominating committee members should serve no more than two consecutive years. They should represent different interests, different ages, different friends. Their instructions should be: Find the most interested, enthusiastic, responsible and hard-working members to serve on the board; and don't select nominees all from one "faction" within the organization.

Nominating committees must take their responsibilities seriously. They must ask questions of the members and get ideas. The committee, of course, will nominate some long-time, hard-working members, but they should also come up with other candidates who have little to write about in a "profile" but who have spark and new ideas. If these eager new people must wait until they have worked their way up with impressive credentials, the organization is likely to find that these members have gone elsewhere where they can more quickly use their leadership talents.

Most organizations hold their elections at the annual meeting. (The ballots are counted or the results announced, or the vote is actually taken.) The new president takes over at the following meeting. The annual meeting is the time for the president to do an extra-warm job of expressing appreciation for the fine work done by each person who played a special part in the organization that year. Sometimes that hard-working, outgoing president is forgotten. The board certainly should remember to recognize the contributions of the retiring leader, but if for some reason that is neglected, the new president should make a special comment at the next meeting. Whatever happens, the outgoing president should realize that the hard work and frustrations were nothing compared to the privilege of being able to lead the group. If the membership is mired in many activities at the annual meeting and forgets to give proper thanks, it doesn't mean they don't appreciate their leader's contributions.

Praise, recognition and thanks are important to all of us, but if people forget, consider it a small matter. Good work was certainly noted, even if only silently. The important matter now is that the president find ways to recognize and give appreciation to each member who contributed to a good year. Let the president never forget that without the members, nothing good could have been done!

(Sample annual letter)

---

HELPING HAND COUNCIL
444 West Cannon Street
Grand Junction, Mass.

Sept. 10, 1981

Dear Members:

This year's ANNUAL MEETING of the Helping Hand Council will be held Wednesday, October 7 at 7:30 p.m. in the Red Cross Building, 444 West Cannon Street, Grand Junction. All members are invited to attend and stay for the meeting of the Board of Directors, which will follow.

Once again, we are conducting the election of new officers and directors by mail. Please fill out the enclosed ballot and return it in the enclosed envelope so that we receive it by October 6. Note that a space has been provided for write-in votes.

The Board of Directors is composed of four officers and twelve directors. Officers are elected yearly for one-year terms, and may serve no more than two years in any one office. Half the directors are elected each year for two-year terms, and they cannot serve consecutively for more than two terms (total of four years) as directors.

The Council's nominating committee prepared the attached slate. A brief profile of each nominee is provided on another sheet. Please indicate your choices by checking the appropriate spaces or by write-in votes on the appropriate lines.

We hope to see you at the meeting. In the meantime, please don't forget to vote!

Sincerely,


Elizabeth Deane
President

(Sample ballot)

---

## 1981 NOMINATIONS FOR OFFICERS AND DIRECTORS

OFFICERS:   (Vote for ONE person for each office)

Chair:       ___ Ms. Sarah Tracey

               ___ _____ (write in)

Vice-chair:  ___ Dr. Robert Jackson

               ___ _____ (write in)

Secretary:   ___ Mr. Graham Bryant

               ___ _____ (write in)

Treasurer:   ___ Dr. Grace Demersky

               ___ _____ (write in)

DIRECTORS: (Vote for SIX)

            ___ Mr. William Carey

            ___ Ms. Nancy Evans

            ___ Mr. Albert Greene

            ___ Dr. John Hoekstra

            ___ Mr. Peter McVeen

            ___ Ms. Mary Rothingham

            **(write in)**

_____

_____

_____

_____

_____

_____

**(Note: Attach profiles of your nominees to your ballot)**

# Officers and Directors

ORGANIZATION LEADERSHIP IS ordinarily composed of four officers and a board of directors. This chapter outlines the duties of leaders and offers some suggestions to help keep things running smoothly and efficiently.

### The President

A firm piece of advice: Bylaws should limit a president to serving no more than two years. Perhaps you will argue that your organization is an exception, but it's a good bet that after two years a hard-working, unpaid president won't want to serve another term. A weak president, on the other hand, may be willing to serve forever. After all, he or she enjoys the compliment of a continued presidency with very little effort. The volunteer organization has everything to gain and little to lose by imposing strict limitations on the length of service of all its officers. Thus leadership is rotated; new ideas keep coming to the top; dead wood is cut with no embarrassment; the organization stays lively.

### The Vice-President

The vice-president presides when the president is absent. That is about the only clear rule for vice-presidents. Some organizations decide that the vice-president should take on another specific duty, often program chair. This can be a troublesome policy. It is healthy to require that the vice-president take on some duty, because vice-presidents are usually offered the presidency eventually and it is wise to know that the vice-president is willing to work. However, the vice-president's time and talents don't always fit a special duty the organization specifies in its bylaws.

Your choices for vice-president will be limited if your bylaws specify a responsibility attached to the position. For instance, perhaps your group wants a certain woman for vice-president, but she's too busy at the moment to take on a big responsibility. She promises a large commitment for the following year, perhaps as president, but makes it clear that the year of the vice-presidency is largely committed to something else.

Or, you may merely want a vice-president to provide a dash of prestige or expertise, someone to represent the organization well and whose thinking will be of value on the board of directors. This person is willing to serve as vice-president but has no interest in being president. Again, you might lose your first choice for the vice-presidency if it has been established as a large job.

Make the vice-presidency flexible. It is your most flexible position, the place where special needs of the organization can be fitted in each year. You might make it a tradition that the vice-president is always asked to be program chair, for instance, but everyone should know that this is not a *requirement* of the office. Or you might want to specify in the bylaws that the vice-president must accept *some* responsibility. The point to remember is that you don't want to limit your options by making the vice-presidency more structured than it needs to be.

### The Secretary

Mixed groups are finally beginning to realize that secretaries don't have to be women. Furthermore, whoever does the job, the secretary's position is important and ought to be so regarded by whoever accepts it. An outstanding woman leader I know once wrote to a friend, "Don't be insulted if you are asked to be secretary. I have been secretary many times, and I have always regarded it as an opportunity. After all, by covering special subjects in special detail—by emphasizing particular areas—the secretary can be very powerful. You do not ever want to misuse power, but as secretary you can (should) legitimately make sure that what you feel *needs* to be especially well covered by the minutes *is* adequately covered."

Secretaries with a good sense of humor can write delightful minutes. If the group isn't too serious, light-hearted comments can be inserted to make the minutes more fun (and hence more likely to be read):

> Tom Greene advised that since coho salmon have the habit of coming apart at the seams when they return to spawn, he felt snagging them could be justified. Malotti so moved and Greene seconded the motion. Greene and Malotti voting yes. Ruhl and Smith voting no. Jones shouting no. Motion failed.

Of great importance is that the minutes be accurate. If the organization conducts complicated business, the secretary can ask the person making a motion to write it down. Accuracy also increases if the secretary phones the people who are paraphrased in the minutes to make sure that each statement is accurate. Another procedure is for the secretary to read (or send) draft minutes to the president ahead of the next meeting, in time to make corrections. Additional corrections can be made during the next meeting when the minutes are approved.

### The Treasurer

It's no wonder that the treasurer's job is often the hardest position to fill. Most people hate to take care of their own checkbooks, let alone that of an organization. But good treasurers can be found. Likely candidates are people retired from business, well-organized homemakers, accountants and bookkeepers. Important qualifications should be that they know something about keeping books, have time to do the job, and are known to be responsible. Whoever is chosen to be treasurer, there are three important actions your organization can take to make sure that your treasury is cared for properly.

First, somebody with a knowledge of simple bookkeeping should look at the books and make sure they are set up so that anyone can, after simple explanation, work with them.

Second, despite the group's continual difficulties in finding a treasurer, and the unlikely possibility that you may be able to find a gem who might be willing to continue forever, *a treasurer should serve no more than two years*. A constant change of treasurers insures that no major problems—from inattention, carelessness, ignorance, or even temptation—creep into the bookkeeping.

Third, there should be an annual audit without fail. If it isn't feasible to hire an auditor, a three-member committee may be appointed. This committee will have the responsibility of going over the bills, checks, tax forms, books and bank accounts to make sure that everything is in good order. (In case a problem is discovered, it's much easier for a three-person team to ask the treasurer about it than for the responsibility to be placed on one member.)

The annual audit is protection for the treasurer as well as the group. Volunteer groups are often careless about their money and their books, and then vaguely get the idea that there should be more money in the treasury than there actually is. The treasurer should be protected by clear approval at the end of each year. In fact, no prospective treasurer should take the job if the organization won't make sure that the books are audited in a businesslike manner at the end of each year.

For both the group and the new treasurer, probably the greatest service the annual audit provides is protection against sloppy bookkeeping. Many of us have been in volunteer organizations when someone finally pointed out that, over the years, the books have become an absolute mess. Income tax forms weren't filed; accounts weren't clear; sometimes even old bills remained unpaid. In such instances it takes endless amounts of time to straighten things out.

Sloppy bookkeeping in volunteer organizations is an invitation to other problems too, such as the treasurer who forgets to return cash borrowed from the treasury (despite the fact that money should *never* be borrowed from the treasury), or who mixes up household moneys with organization moneys. Most of us have heard some tale about someone actually walking off with the club purse, but that is rare. The problem seldom is one of conscious dishonesty. When it arises, the problem is usually a human one—the same sort of thing that happens to many of us when we try to keep our own checkbooks straight. No matter how innocent such problems are, they must be promptly corrected.

Besides the annual audit, the organization should develop written guidelines for the care of its treasury. These guidelines should be kept in the notebooks of all the officers and be part of the bylaws. The guidelines should include:

1. There shall be an annual audit at the end of each fiscal year, with a report back to the organization.

2. The auditors may go over the books with the treasurer, but the full audit must be done privately.

3. Receipts shall be given for all membership dues and contributions, and shall be recorded in the club books.

4. The club shall develop a budget for all its committees and functions, and no amount over $(_____) shall be spent without the approval of the board of directors.

5. When a large amount of cash is received at meetings and events, at least one other person, appointed by the president, shall help the treasurer receive the money and count it.

6. No such money shall be counted privately. It will be counted at the meeting or event, the amount announced to everyone remaining, and the amount

recorded both in the secretary's minutes and the treasurer's books.

7. Cash shall not be kept longer than overnight or weekends (other than $_____ for petty cash).

8. The bank shall be informed that the policy of the club is that no checks may be withdrawn to "cash."

9. There shall be a monthly and a full annual treasurer's report, and these reports will be kept in both the secretary's and the treasurer's books.

To sum up: Take the treasury seriously. Select as your treasurer a person who is not a stranger to keeping books. No matter how good your treasurer when you do find one, change treasurers every two years. Set up your books so they are simple to keep. Make sure that there are regular reports and audits, and that your guidelines for the treasurer are strictly followed.

Then relax. With those procedures your treasury will never get far out of hand.

### The Directors

In most organizations, directors and officers work together to set policy for the organization. New ideas and actions are approved by them and they oversee the general operation of the entire organization. Usually each has a vote except the president, who votes only to break a tie, or in special cases, to *make* a tie. (See Rules chapter.)

There are two methods of obtaining directors. Most often they are elected by the members. However, some organization bylaws state that some of the directors sit on the board by virtue of a particular representation or chair. Such directors are usually appointed, not elected.

When the bylaws mandate that a committee chairperson serve on the board, those bylaws should also permit that chairperson to designate a committee member to represent him. It is nonproductive to saddle a committee chair with another burden if someone else would serve more enthusiastically.

The most productive volunteer organizations are usually those groups that keep down the number of directors. It is virtually impossible for a president to maintain communications with a large governing body, and the conduct of business becomes unwieldy. I believe that sixteen members, including the four officers, is the maximum number for getting work done efficiently.

All directors, like the officers, should be limited by the bylaws in the time they may serve. Organizations get into a rut they can hardly extricate themselves from if they don't set limits to service. Member loyalty or kindness makes it too hard to "bounce" a sincere, interested director after he or she has served for several years. I suggest a limit of two consecutive two-year terms, for a total of four years. An effective member can continue to serve, if elected, by taking an office. (Conversely, an officer can serve further as a member of the board.) The limitation on the time a person can serve in a particular position insures that leadership changes and that the organization has the opportunity to bring new, creative people into the leadership circle. Strong, active members still have the opportunity to serve in other capacities, and to come back on the board a year later.

Finally, remember that the purpose of a board of directors is to set policy and oversee the organization's progress and action. Committee action, for instance, must be approved by the board. To keep your organization lively and moving, you must be creative, innovative, responsive and responsible. Directors chosen merely for their loyalty, financial contribution, or length of service, will mean a board that is dead on its feet. That's a dead organization. You want *yours* alive and kicking.

# Why Reinvent
# the Wheel?

I F YOUR ORGANIZATION is typical, each new officer and each new committee chair is expected to know—by some mysterious means—what his or her responsibilities are and how to carry them out. Few instructions are given verbally; written instructions are non-existent; written information, if it exists, is in disarray. There is no organized attempt to pass along what you know; instructions and background information must be painfully reacquired year after year.

The new secretary learns he is supposed to send the minutes to the president only when the aggrieved president calls and asks why she didn't receive them. The program chair lacks information about the cost of renting an auditorium, needs the addresses and telephone numbers of your favorite speakers, wonders what printing company you used last year.

Most leaders muddle along the best they can, doing half a job, putting up with endless grief. Those who work hard to find the information they need do so at the expense of time that could be spent getting the job done. What a waste of time and energy! What a waste of human resources.

Not only do organizations neglect to share and pass on information within the group, but they also fail to appreciate the importance of sharing information with other groups. Groups are surprised to discover how much they

91

can help each other and save time when they develop a method of communication.

This chapter addresses both of these neglected matters: passing on information within the organization and sharing information with groups outside your own. It is to help you avoid reinventing the wheel.

### Passing Along Information within the Organization

Any member responsible for an activity needs a clear description of his or her duties. I don't think it is necessary (in fact, I think it is counterproductive) for volunteer organizations to do somersaults writing detailed "goals and objectives." (In management jargon, that means broad goals and specific, short-term ones.) Instead, I believe it is only important to give the general purpose of the task, and state as concisely and briefly as possible what the duties are, and then to provide other information that has been gathered from past efforts. The purpose is to help members perform their duties with a minimum of unnecessary effort.

Here a caveat is in order: Once an organization sets down this information, it is in danger of eventually becoming rigid. It seems to be human to codify ideas and decide that just because something has been done one way, it must always be done in the same way. That is why new organizations are often more creative and effective than older ones. Therefore, spell out the duties as simply as possible so you leave breathing space for creative ideas. Creativity is so important that I advise including with every job description something like the following:

**Note: Please feel free to offer new suggestions to improve the way your committee functions, or to change direction. If you cannot perform one of the duties listed, discuss with the president how the matter might be handled.**

My advice in this book isn't set in concrete. I hope your job descriptions won't be, either. In voluntary organizations, talents and interests constantly change. It is important to insist that necessary housekeeping duties be performed. Minutes must be kept; money must be raised. And certain restrictions and demands may be necessary to ensure your organization's credibility. But that does not mean that most jobs must be done in the same manner year after year. Nor is it necessary that the group always carry on the same projects.

For instance, what the energy committee does depends on the interests and talents of the individual chairperson and committee members. The stated purpose for the energy committee is to help promote alternatives to the use of scarce resources, and in using energy, to protect the environment. This is a broad goal that can encompass many kinds of projects. Perhaps the past chairperson was big on recycling and started a successful community recycling program. The new chair is an engineer strongly interested and knowledgeable in the subject of solar energy. In the best of all organizations, the recycling committee has spun off from the energy committee (or remains as an active, special project within the energy committee) and the new energy chair uses his resources to develop community interest and education in solar energy.

To use another example: In a women's liberation organization, the past publicity chair had a flair for projects that dramatized women's problems. The new chair prefers to develop and distribute educational literature to persuade the community in a different manner. Or the new chair is a creative person with no preconceived ideas, but initiates great plans for action as issues develop.

Allow for the development of new strategies. Purposes, duties, background information, should be given to help members, not put them in a strait jacket.

This is the kind of information you need to provide:

1. General purpose of the office or committee. (Bylaws of your organization may spell this out. In any case, include a copy.)

2. Duties of the officer or chairperson. (Just what are his or her responsibilities? Are there deadlines to be met? What other details should he know? To whom must reports be given? Is the person expected to attend board meetings?)

3. Any information that makes it easier to do the job, such as:

   • Company addresses and telephone numbers

   • Prices

   • Reminders for specific projects. (See, for example, the checklist at the end of the program chapter.)

   • Ideas for projects

   • Suggested strategies

   • Past projects and how they were handled. What worked, and what didn't

   • Resource persons inside and outside the organization (with addresses and telephone numbers)

In the fund-raising chapter, I suggest that, upon completion of a project, the ways and means committee meet to discuss and write down information that may help in future projects. All committees will be well served if they also do this. But—again—avoid getting overly involved with paperwork. Nothing infuriates most effective volunteers more than having to fill out forms.

### How to Help Your Organization Pass Along Information

If the kind of help I have been talking about is not already available to your members, how do you develop it? Anyone in the group can suggest that it be done and offer to get the work started. Probably, however, the president will take the initiative. Whoever does it begins by collecting whatever instructions are available—from bylaws, from past chairpersons.

Then he or she asks the previous (or continuing) officers and chairs to list what they perceive their duties were (or are) and gather any other information that will help people perform their jobs efficiently. (Unfortunately, most of your chairpersons will probably ignore this request.) The next step is for the president—or whoever is in charge of this project—to get together with at least one other person, perhaps the vice-president, to develop a general definition, or purpose, for each office and committee and to list their responsibilities. This can be done in consultation with past presidents, new officers, old and new chairpersons. Note that some of the definitions and duties will already be defined in the bylaws.

File folders, looseleaf notebooks, index card files— all are ways to keep such information. The persons working on the project can decide how best to present it. In addition, scrap books should be given to the publicity committee and ways and means committee so they may keep a record of press releases, clippings, etc. If you are lucky, your organization already has much of the information you need; you will only need to update and organize it. If, however, a great deal of information was turned over to some of your hapless committee chairs in disorganized batches and boxes, the best you may do is simply ask your chairs to organize it however they can, and start fresh with newer information.

When the work is done, the president or project chair (in consultation with the president) should write a definition of purpose for any office or committee that has not already been defined in the bylaws. These should go to the board of directors with a note that if they have any problems with the definitions of purpose, they should contact the president. Some may need to be reworded. If there is disagreement over what a committee's purpose should be, that matter must be taken up at a meeting of your board.

Try not to make this project a major event, or it is bound to get overorganized. After all, you are only trying to improve a process. The language and specified duties can be clarified, changed and improved from then on.

Finally, an addendum to my advice about passing on your information: Be sure your organization has a historian who keeps up your archives. It is amazing how many groups fail to keep a good record of their past. Make sure your organization keeps a scrapbook up to date (even though newspaper clippings may be duplicated by various committees). Newsletters, minutes, treasury reports, bylaws, and other documents should be kept in binders. Otherwise, they get lost. You also need a chronological record of the names of all past officers, directors and chairpersons, as well as the activities of your organization. Most such information is buried in other documents; for easy reference, keep a separate record.

All your books should be well marked in two places on the covers: "Return to (your organization)" with an address you can use indefinitely. In case future members get sloppy and forget about their records, or your archivist moves away or dies, you will more likely get those records returned. They are important. They, too, will save endless time hunting for information.

### Sharing Information with Other Groups

Organizations too often grope for information that is readily available from other groups. They also duplicate each other's services. They spread themselves thin when they could concentrate on what they do best. They try to develop experts within their own group when it might be more sensible to use expertise from other organizations. They bring a program speaker from across the country, not knowing that somebody in the community is more qualified and perhaps more entertaining. They work on legislation not knowing that other groups have contacts that could help them.

Organizations will save time and perform more effectively if they communicate with other groups about their activities.

Once your organization begins to communicate, you will discover many ways you can help one another. In our community, the local TB and Emphysema Society offered space, computer, and mail sorting services upon learning the needs of a fledgling group concerned with air pollution. Several agencies and groups provide leadership training courses for volunteers. Groups learned that more than fifty people in the community were paid to help volunteers; yet their services were unknown to most of the community, and many of the services overlapped.

The public library kept a speakers' file for use by program chairpersons. Few people knew about it; the file was seldom used, and the library had trouble keeping the file current. The Chamber of Commerce had a list of volunteer groups in the community—an invaluable aid to other groups—but again, it was underused and incomplete. The groups also learned that a number of organizations provide free space for meetings.

By getting together, by "networking," you can— among other things—learn just what services are available. If some needed services aren't offered, groups will be encouraged to provide them. A busy organization may feel hard-pressed to spend extra time working with other groups. The time spent networking, however, can be invaluable.

In fact, because more and more groups are learning the importance of sharing information and working together for a cause, many are creating formal councils. The shared expertise and knowledge, and the compromise solutions, translate into broad influence and effectiveness.

### How to Start an Informal Network of Organizations

It is easy to reach out and maintain contact with other groups. Somebody simply has to be interested enough to initiate communications. A few inquiries may turn up a list of organizations similar to your group. Otherwise, the inquiries will help you develop your own list. You may also discover a communications network is already in existence. You'll want to participate.

If you must start from scratch, develop a telephone and mailing list and call the organization presidents, following up with a letter. Invite them (or ask them to send a representative) to join you at an informal lunch or breakfast meeting. Tell them that the purpose is to get to know one another and learn more about each other's groups, and to see if there are ways you might be useful to one another. Probably you will need to tell them that each will pay his own way. Most people will be pleased to come.

Keep your first meeting informal and friendly. Don't try for a formal agenda. It is only important to ask each person to introduce himself or herself and say something about his group. Suggest that if they have needs that one of the other groups might be able to give some help on, please feel free to mention it. As discussion develops, people will begin to offer each other ideas and assistance.

By the end of the meeting, be sure to ask if people would like to meet again; then decide together on a time and place. How matters evolve from there depends on many ingredients, but remember that each group has its own priorities.

Be aware, too, that if groups differ on a racial, ethnic, class, age or other "label" basis, or if they perceive themselves to be in competition—or any other reason—everyone will need to make special efforts to build the trust that is essential for a cooperative working relationship.

For instance, be sure any agendas are developed in cooperation with representatives from every group involved.

What if no one in your group has the time to initiate the kind of network I have been discussing? You might want to contact one of the volunteer agencies, groups, or individuals in your community who may be interested in the idea and do the work. A "Y" or central volunteer agency is an important contact. Either may be more than happy to be of assistance.

Also, after your group gets started, someone must be responsible for making calls or writing letters to keep people informed and involved. One of these agencies may be willing to take over the load.

Each group will have the responsibility of finding somebody interested enough and free enough to represent their members on a continuing basis. It is good if someone high in their leadership can participate. Otherwise, they should prevail upon a past president or other interested member who can share their organization's knowledge and bring back useful information to their members.

Networking: a surprisingly useful tool.

I conclude this chapter by bringing you back to my original point. That is, when we neglect to share our information with others, people must learn, by trial and error, that which is already known. If we can avoid it, why reinvent the wheel?

# Part III:

# Effective Leaders

# So You've Been Chosen As Our Leader

IN A VOLUNTEER organization, anyone who shows an interest, volunteers to work, and isn't too critical of fellow members, will rise quickly to a leadership position. There aren't that many hard-working volunteers. Sometimes it's simply a matter of being pleasant and present to get to be president.

There are two kinds of presidents. One accepts merely for the honor. The organization begins to die a little while that kind of president is in office. The other kind of president takes his or her responsibilities seriously and does everything possible to help the organization go forward.

What are some of the goals of a good president?

- to make people glad to be part of the organization
- to make people want to participate
- to see that the work of the organization gets done, through his own efforts and by the work of the other officers, committee chairs and enthusiastic members.

There are hidden talents and interests in any group, and leaders have a great opportunity to make the most of these abilities. Therein lies a problem; there is no financial incentive for anyone to work, and most volunteer leaders don't have the skills, training or experience to know how to do the job. It is remarkable that volunteer leaders do as well as they do, but it would be easier if they had some guidelines and pointers. That is what this chapter is all about.

The first rule for the new leader is to start out on the right foot—with a smile and at least a pretense of self-assurance. Have you ever listened to a new and obviously nervous committee chair or president apologize for being nervous? It spoils the whole effect. From then on, the listeners are watching for signs of nervousness and paying less attention to what is said.

It isn't unusual to be nervous, and stage fright isn't reserved for the inexperienced. I've watched the president of a state professional society visibly shake as he gave a simple talk before a luncheon group, and I've seen experienced politicians fumble with the pages they were reading because their hands were shaking so hard. None of us, no matter how experienced, is immune to shyness or insecurity, so why should someone new on the job apologize for being human?

The point is, don't apologize. Realize that everyone shares your feelings from time to time, and when your goofs are noticeable, others will be sympathetic. If you apologize, you will surely disappoint your audience. Soldiers who win medals for bravery aren't asked whether their knees were shaking when they went into battle. After all, one reason you were chosen was because people figured you were brave enough to do the job.

Next, you must decide to be prepared. If you can't spend the time to organize the agenda for each meeting, you shouldn't have taken the job. Throughout your term of office you must organize, work hard, keep priorities in mind, and take your responsibilities seriously.

Finally, you must help your members participate fully. *Save enough thinking time to figure out where you need help and who can give it. Don't try to do everything yourself.*

Good leadership is less a matter of techniques than a matter of understanding. You know you need enthusiastic participation and effort on the part of your members. To have that you must make sure that your organization is doing what its members want it to do. If the leadership pushes programs and projects, however noble, in which nobody is really interested, members aren't going to participate. We are talking about people's free time, freely given.

Unless their ideas are unacceptable to the organization, committees should choose their own goals and projects. The organization as a whole chooses the general goals, but make sure they are goals for which there are workers. I once belonged to a group that every year chose the same laudatory goal. And every year nobody signed up to do the work.

Once people get in gear, they are going to need appreciation and recognition for their efforts. Participation will be far more enthusiastic if there is some positive feedback. The president should sincerely appreciate efforts of each and every participating member, and let the other members know what is being done. No meeting should go by without acknowledgement that Mary Smith is working hard on the building fund and will present a report shortly, or that Paul Peters and his committee have worked hard on the petition drive. You have to walk a fine line between making a meeting tedious with reports and fully recognizing the efforts of the members. (Remember, however, that every time you give a chairperson a chance to report, you're also giving leadership experience.)

If the organization is active and meeting time is limited, the president may simply acknowledge the work in progress each month, unless a committee needs to discuss a matter with the entire membership. Make sure that the committees have a chance to report from time to time in your newsletter. If even that is unworkable, then a report from them at the end of the year is a must.

Throughout this book I mention hurt feelings, appreciation and involvement, because volunteer groups can only survive on the good will and enthusiasm of their members. I can't remind you often enough that people are there because they get satisfaction out of being in the group—

socially, intellectually, or because they feel committed to a good cause. If you can't satisfy their needs, they will go elsewhere.

### People Problems

Despite the various—and not always helpful—personalities of your members, you must cheerfully determine to do your best to understand them and work with them. All kinds of people join organizations. Besides the brightest and the best, there are the dullards, the talkers, the critics, the neurotics, the gossips and the overly sensitive. Real leaders don't get hung up on the faults of members. Instead, they appreciate members' potential. All persons have contributions to make. Try to control the excesses, and ignore what you can't control. The most annoying people are usually the most lonely, unappreciated, insecure and unsatisfied. Spend some time thinking about how their talents can be put to use. Listen to what they have to say. Good ideas don't come only from great personalities.

You have probably already learned that when people complain that something ought to be done, you can turn their complaints into a suggestion that they handle the problem. This takes the responsibility off your overworked back, and it helps to quiet the chronic complainer. Sometimes you will get a response of real assistance.

If you consistently look for opportunities to give your most troublesome people responsibility, you may be surprised to find that they not only make a genuine contribution, but that they also become happier members of the group. It is exciting to discover untapped resources; people are our greatest untapped resource.

You may also have members who take up too much of your personal time outside the meeting. For instance, you give a job to someone who needed involvement and recognition, but his reaction to getting attention becomes a serious demand on your time and patience. If you find yourself going overboard at the expense of yourself and those around you, talk to yourself: "*I* have needs, too. My family has needs. I am working for this organization, as is this person. We must both do our part to help. This person is hurting me. I must put an end to it."

When you come to that conclusion, you do something about the situation—straightforwardly and without guilt. Always try to be kind, but also be honest and sensible with yourself and others. When you don't have time to talk, say so. When people begin to "report in," or ask your advice too often, or rehash old problems, tell them that your time is so limited you'll have to depend on them to carry on. When that doesn't work, be very firm. If that causes hurt feelings, you've done your best, and it is up to them to decide whether to keep on working or quit.

### Getting Members Involved

The president should stay on the lookout for fresh ideas and new workers, and look for opportunities to bring them out. One of the greatest resources that organizations often neglect is retired people, who have time to give and valuable experience behind them. Keep your eye out, too, for people who stay in the background and never volunteer. If you tell them what is needed, they may turn out to be your most willing and enthusiastic workers. Anyone who continues to appear at meetings, or who tentatively offers ideas or help, should be sounded out and found a place. These people are often gems. Once started, there may be no end to their contributions in time, talent and personality.

It helps to let the group know your unfulfilled needs. Some of your shyer members will then volunteer. (Keep in close touch with your committee chairs so you *know* all your needs.) If possible, start by sending out a written plea at the beginning of the organization year. (Whenever you want a response, send along return envelopes.) List all your needs with spaces to check, and add an item: "Additional suggestions or work you would be willing to do," with plenty of space for response. Throughout the year, encourage your committee chairs to make announcements regarding the help they need, and continue to remind people they are needed. Be as specific as possible about smaller jobs begging to be filled.

Sometimes people volunteer, but catch you when you have your mind on a million other things; you forget to follow through. To avoid losing a worker or causing a misunderstanding, periodically comment to the group that if you have forgotten to contact someone who has volunteered—please volunteer again!

Keep trying to find the right niche for each of your members. Listen carefully to what they have to say, and try to be aware of their interests. There are so many matters that a frazzled president ends up doing at the last minute: addressing envelopes, greeting people, making coffee, cleaning up, managing the archives, writing thank-you letters. Take the time to give a little foresight to what your needs are. You will be able to find people who would be delighted to help if asked.

On the other hand, a caution is in order. Remember that not everybody wants to, or can, participate. They may have other demands on their time and energies. Respect this and don't be pushy. No one should feel obligated to participate. It is enough that they support the group and want to come. Your job is to encourage—but not insist upon—participation.

When you are working on ways to get more done and involve more people, don't forget the telephone committee, for all kinds of emergencies and for getting people out for special events. A "carpenter committee" can make needed objects like a portable bookcase or a podium. A "library committee" can bring, organize and oversee books for the membership to exchange.

Be flexible when new people get involved. They may want to be helpful, yet be reluctant to tell you that they really don't like the job you suggest. If a twinge of pain crosses the face of someone when he hears your suggestion, offer a different one. If someone takes on a job but later indicates that whatever he is doing isn't very satisfying, try to find him another spot.

One of my most endearing examples is a retired woman who volunteered to be an "office volunteer"—that is, she answered the phone and did whatever was needed around the office. It soon became evident, however, that she was frustrated by typing and filing; she didn't feel competent. She finally quit, but in the meantime her quiet charm and intelligence had had a chance to be noticed. We put her on the board of directors, and eventually she accepted an office. It wasn't until long after all this had happened that we learned she was a renowned scientist whose former work continues to save the lives of thousands of children.*

You can't expect to "discover" many people like that, but you can expect to broaden member participation and get to know and enjoy many people who are special to you because you've gotten to know them better. Stay alert and interested, and you will create an atmosphere in which people will feel welcome to offer new suggestions and their services.

I give you two illustrations of what I mean:

In a busy organization a timid, retiring, elderly woman was the only person who responded to a request for suggestions. At the end of the meeting she hesitantly took the president aside and pointed out that the group was beginning to attract some younger people, and that it would be nice to serve punch as well as coffee. This was a kind, thoughtful idea that busier members had overlooked, but that did indeed mean a great deal to the young members.

The other example illustrates the significant role any single member can play. During the passage of Michigan's

---

*This was Dr. Grace Eldering, who with her senior partner, Dr. Pearl Kendrick, developed the first successful whooping cough vaccine, a vaccine still in use throughout the world. When the vaccine was developed, whooping cough killed more infants than all other diseases combined. At the time of this writing, these women remain virtually unknown.

Environmental Protection Act, supporters knew it was necessary that citizens attend legislative sessions to demonstrate strong citizen interest. One of the people urged to attend was an unassuming member who couldn't be very active in the group but who had shown great interest in the organization's goals. It was a coincidence that she had once done part-time secretarial work for one of the legislators. When she observed the typical last-minute attempts to weaken the bill by damaging amendments, she decided to act. She got her old boss out of the legislative session and told him why he should vote against an especially damaging amendment. He was persuaded. He went back to his seat and voted against the amendment, and *it was defeated by one vote*.

That bill, as enacted into legislation, has been considered a model for other states around the country. One unassuming person played a key role in its passage. *Never underestimate the importance of each and every one of your members.* Remember the slogan: **"None of us is as smart as all of us."**

# Keeping Committees Alive and Well

**A** VITAL DUTY of the president is to keep important committees alive and well. When you take office, committee chairpersons must be appointed. Don't underestimate the importance of wise selection, for these will be the people responsible for carrying out the work of your organization.

First, learn which committee chairs have been doing a good job. Unless they want to change or you want to appoint somebody promising fresh ideas and equal work, you'll reappoint the old chairperson.

Other chairpersons will present problems to you, and a few pointers are in order. Just about every organization has a hard working chair who has been in a job too long; members are no longer satisfied with the work the person is doing. Often the result is gossip, hard feelings and organizational turmoil. How you handle these kinds of problems will tell much about your leadership abilities.

Look at the problem calmly and reasonably. Are people being critical, but no one else is willing to step in and do a thankless job? If so, tell the critics that until they find you an equally hard-working chair, they had better appreciate the one they have.

I believe it is terribly important to try to avoid hurting a hard-working volunteer's feelings, yet still resolve the problem. One way is to appoint a parallel committee with a different title to get going in another direction. The work can be divided sensibly, and the old chairperson can continue to contribute. Another way is to give that person a new job.

If you have someone to take the chair's place, and strongly believe that appointing a new person is the best route, be honest. Express your gratitude for the good work done, but admit that you think that it isn't good for one person to stay in the same job year after year. Ask your chair to take a different job, which you specify. Also ask him to help the new chairperson get started. Sometimes this results in miffed feelings, but most people know in their hearts that volunteer leadership needs to change periodically and will be gracious if their contributions are, and continue to be, appreciated.

You have a different problem if your chair takes actions despite the stated opposition of his committee or your directors: Feel no hesitancy about replacing him. Tell him or her you appreciate his dedication, but everyone has to work together and majority has to rule. Replace the chair and then proceed as if the matter never happened. The world doesn't revolve around these temporary organizational difficulties, and the less you make of them, the smoother all the transitions will go.

All important committees should be examined. It does no one any good to reappoint a chairperson to an important committee if the job isn't getting done. At the beginning of the organization year, appoint somebody else. Usually a chair realizes he isn't performing well. It's likely he was talked into taking a job and thinks that his weak efforts are better than nothing. By appointing someone else, the president does him and the group a favor. (On the other hand, some chairs like to be around and feel involved, even though they know they aren't very useful. The president can hope to make them feel just as involved by giving them less demanding responsibilities.)

Sometimes the problem of not getting a job done lies with an elected treasurer or secretary, rather than an appointed chair. Minutes and treasurer's reports *must* be written monthly. When a treasurer or secretary gets behind one month, the president must speak to him or her immediately to make sure the work will be caught up before the next month. If it happens again, ask the officer if he needs a replacement. If he says no, tell him that you will have to ask the board to elect a replacement if the reports aren't forthcoming by the third month. You can appreciate a person's problems while still remaining firm about the legitimate needs of your organization.

In all such "people problem" cases, be kind and friendly, but also firm and reasonable toward both the people involved and your group. Don't blow people problems out of proportion, but do something before small difficulties become major sources of dissension among members.

One of the worst mistakes leaders make is to talk someone into taking a job when that person doesn't have the time or interest. If someone indicates a genuine reluctance about being able to do a good job, and it's not a case of modesty or shyness, take him at his word. Admit that you need an active chair, and don't press further. Fit people's needs, abilities, and interests in with your needs. The strength and activities of organizations change over the years, depending on the talents and time of its members. Your job is to emphasize the strengths and do the best you can with the weaknesses.

If you wind up with a committee and no chairperson, decide whether it can be dropped for a year. If it is necessary to keep the committee alive, try to find someone who will accept a limited responsibility, such as keeping up on legislation regarding the committee's subject and informing the members what they can do. Let the other members know the agreement you have made, stating that the present chairperson would be happy for someone else to volunteer for the job of chair. That eliminates the complainers and protects your chairperson. If others are eager to get more accomplished, the responsibility is squarely up to them.

Sometimes an active committee chair is intensely interested and hard-working, but strictly a loner; the committee is memberless. I don't like the idea of co-chairing because it often doesn't work well; co-chairs have a hard time working out and separating responsibilities. Nevertheless, this may be the only kind way to get more participation for an important job. If the president can define specific areas of responsibility to each of them, the arrangement can work. For instance, one might be charged with "special projects" or "research," and the other charged with "committee action."

Once in awhile you'll be pleased to hear that someone is especially concerned about a particular problem your group cares about, and you have no committee handling the problem. Rush to see if he or she will chair a new committee.

A word of caution, however: Many an enthusiastic president loses the chance to get an activity moving because the president has a larger concept than the volunteer. Be careful; don't overwhelm your prospect with your own grand ideas. Instead, let the member tell you what he or she has in mind. Ask for help getting the job done. You may only be able to convince the person to research the subject; that alone can be a significant start in providing the information needed for others to begin work; and as the member learns, it may encourage him to volunteer for the next necessary steps.

The reverse situation is also common. You hear from a volunteer with a much larger concept for action than you have. Resist the temptation to say why the idea won't work. If you think it poses major difficulties, suggest starting on a limited basis. Keep your attitude positive and open, no matter how screwy or impractical you think the idea is. Give that person a fair chance to get a full hearing. Do inform him that "the board will want to know . . . " so that he can think about some possible objections, and be prepared. Whenever possible, allow your creative eager beavers to prove themselves. They are often trouble, but they often, too, help an organization move in significant, worthwhile directions.

The only time you can legitimately dismiss new ideas is when your organization has its hands so full doing worthwhile things that one more activity would be a burden it simply cannot handle. There aren't many organizations in that category.

Once you have worked out committee chairmanships and priorities, you do all you can to support and work with your leaders. President Lyndon Johnson's obsession for telephoning congressmen was the subject of a good deal of joking. Nevertheless, until the Vietnam War undermined his effectiveness, Johnson had an amazing ability to get his programs through Congress. A major reason was his keen awareness of a key requirement of leadership: to lead, you need to understand the people working with and for you, and they need to understand you.

Therefore, at least once a month the president should be in touch with every single committee chairperson. The chair who is sought out for ideas, information and feedback is going to be far more interested and involved.

I cannot emphasize enough how important it is to keep in close touch with all those who have leadership jobs in your organization. It is the only way to insure that they continue to be encouraged, that they don't take off in some direction which the organization would oppose, and that you keep yourself informed.

You should also help your chairs find members for their committees. (The previous chapter on leadership deals with this more fully.) A useful technique is to introduce each of your chairpersons in a general meeting and have them say a few words about their committees. Then assign the chairs to different parts of the room, with signs indicating their committee names. Ask everyone who is interested in knowing more about a committee to please move to the designated location. The chairpersons (identified by name tags and the signs, and supplied with pens and paper) can then discuss their subjects more fully and sign up interested workers.

Finally, you can support your committee leaders by sharing the glory. They, not you, should be interviewed about their special committee projects. They, not you, should report to the full organization when detail is needed about their work. Whenever you can give credit and recognize a member for what he or she is doing, you assure continued enthusiasm for getting the work done. People on committees do most of the work of the organization. What you do to strengthen them, strengthens the organization. While you are in office you will receive due recognition, but in the end, you will be successful only if you and everyone else are successful together.

# Board Meetings — Not Meetings of the Bored

**M**UST THE BOARD meetings of volunteers just be hard work? The answer is no. They should also be fun. Although each president has his or her own style in running a meeting, most successful presidents help their members accomplish their goals in an atmosphere of goodwill and cooperation. These leaders *lead*, but they also *share* the leadership.

Sociologists sometimes classify leadership as autocratic, laissez-faire, and democratic. An appraisal of these leadership types is important.

Let's look at the autocrat first. He or she makes decisions in advance and then tries to make the group go along. The result is that members lose interest or rebel. Or he may be an efficiency expert who conducts business so efficiently that all the joy is taken out of the work. Meetings proceed something like this: The president looks at his or her watch and decides that the meeting should last only so long. The agenda is definite. So far so good, except that this leader is caught up in his plan: Committee chairs or board members are expected to make reports with such dispatch (or worse, the president gives the reports for them) and discussion is kept at such a minimum that people wonder why they bothered to come. Members leave the meeting feeling they didn't really participate, and that the organization is proceeding without their total support.

Then there's the *laissez-faire leader,* who gives no direc-

117

tion and expects the group to come up with all the suggestions and answers. The president merely presides without helping the group come to any decisions, without ever
cutting off discussion, without seeming to get anywhere.
This leader can be even more maddening than the autocratic leader. Both are hard on morale.

The *democratic leader* shares the leadership. It is the
leader's job to keep things moving, to clarify problems, to
make sure that necessary information has been gathered, to
pull together ideas, and to get the group to come to a conclusion. But he also allows and encourages other members
to do the same thing.

This kind of leadership means that the president never
makes members' reports for them unless the members can't
be present. And as long as new points are being made, or
members who wish to speak haven't yet expressed their
opinions, he doesn't cut off discussion. Such shared leadership is orderly, and gets somewhere, but members enjoy the
process.

What is exciting about this process is that it provides
the opportunity for new ideas to bubble to the surface. It's
so easy and so typical for a group to talk itself out of doing
anything. Too often someone suggests a new idea, and the
president or other members immediately start pointing out
all the reasons why it won't work. But where cooperation
and a positive attitude persist, the minute people start raising objections to a new idea, the leader, or anyone else may
interject, "We're just brainstorming," or "Let's just brainstorm this idea a minute before we pick it apart." After the
idea has been aired in a positive manner, objections can be
raised.

I don't mean to imply that meetings should be endless. The president has a responsibility not to waste the
members' time. Unnecessary debate or long-winded reports
need to be cut. Democratic leadership simply means that
reasonable and full discussion by everyone is encouraged
and appreciated. There's no doubt that this kind of meeting

takes longer, but the members' satisfaction from being part of the process will mean more to them than the fact that they might have gone home a little sooner.

It is true that some people will object to longer meetings, especially when the board takes up subjects they aren't interested in. Usually those people most eager to have a short business meeting are those who participate very little in the actual work of the organization, and you shouldn't be dismayed by their impatience. There will also be the extremely hard-working members who just don't have time for the give and take and working-out of various organization problems. Accept their limits. You might have them report first and leave, or give their reports for them if they prefer. If the bylaws allow, you may also have them designate someone else to represent them. In all cases, be sympathetic toward the needs and preferences of your various members, but never expect that you'll always be able to satisfy everyone with whom you work.

### The Agenda

A major responsibility of the president is to be organized for the meeting. You should have made calls to all the committees during the past month and know which items of business are important. Always ask the chairs and other board members to let you know before the meeting if they have anything they want on the agenda.

Before the meeting, put together the agenda in writing. It's good to be able to get it out to all the board members ahead of your meeting, as this helps them prepare. If you are too busy to write, copy and mail an agenda, it's helpful to distribute copies at the beginning of the meeting. If you can't even do that, what is *essential* is that you have in your own hands the order of business for the meeting. The agenda should go something like this:

Acknowledgment of guests and introductions

Secretary's report

Treasurer's report

President's announcements

Committee reports:

Ways and Means, Mary Smith: Progress on plans for auction

Education Committee, Jim Johnson: Plans for slide program

Any other business.

The standard procedure of "old business" first and "new business" next doesn't work well at the board meetings of most volunteer organizations. New business is often inseparable from old business, or may be more important. When you arrange your agenda so that the most important business is handled early in the meeting, you make sure that people don't leave or wear out before your most vital subjects are discussed.

### Keeping the Business Moving

If you have long-winded committee chairpersons you may have to limit their reports, and if during discussion you have long-winded members, you can give them "another minute" before you cut them off. Be careful, however. Don't cut people off unnecessarily. If a subject comes up which appears later in the agenda, decide whether the present momentum makes it reasonable to continue the discussion, or whether you should stop them and tell them that the question is out of order. If everyone seems to be walking around a question without getting to a point, call on the respective chairperson and ask him or her to define and clarify the questions. If you get bogged down in unnecessary detail—for instance, in a discussion about what menu to serve for the annual meeting—suggest that the board set a general policy on the subject (in this case, an acceptable price range for the dinner) and let the committee decide the details. Committees often bring up unnecessary matters for board decisions, and board members get unnecessarily involved. That is especially true if the committee chairperson has no committee and expects the board to act as a committee of the whole.

To move the meeting along and be helpful, the leader needs to know something about the discussion likely to develop. You will be most successful if you've been in touch ahead of time with your chairs. Through discussion with them you can advise them of the kinds of questions they should be prepared to answer, the information they should garner, and the fact that they should have in mind as many pros and cons and alternatives as possible. The more prepared the committee is, the less likely ideas will be tabled, discussion muddled, and time wasted.

Nobody is always going to be able to anticipate all the questions and objections, so you shouldn't feel frustrated if a decision is postponed. Better that it be a well-thought-out decision in the end.

When a matter appears to have been fully discussed, but it's unclear whether members have reached a conclusion, a good device is to ask each member to sum up how he feels. When you seek a comment from each member, you get them to come to grips with the problem. It helps, too, for the leader to sum up (briefly) the various points to clarify the issue.

Once there appears to be a consensus, and if a vote is needed, ask if someone will make a motion so the matter can be decided. There is a special technique you can use for problems which are especially troublesome to the group. I call it the "preliminary decision." In most legislatures it is called the "second reading." During the second reading a bill is acted upon as if it were a final vote—with discussion, amendments, and serious voting. It is then passed on into a third reading for another session. The third reading gives the legislature a chance for a new look, to see if they still feel the same way. Often we don't come to grips with a question, or evaluate all the ramifications, until we have actually made a decision.

For major decisions in your organization, or decisions

which seem to perplex the members, the "second reading" is a marvelous technique. If you foresee problems with a decision, suggest that the vote be a "preliminary decision" vote. This may avoid a lot of problems later. Although in any organization members always have the opportunity to ask for a "vote to reconsider," the preliminary decision technique is more graceful and avoids annoyance or confusion. People know they will vote again, and if after making their decision they are uncomfortable with it, they have an opportunity to re-examine the issue.

A problem calling for a different solution is when matters arise that are no particular committee's concern. You know from the quality of the discussion (arguing, endless debate, unfamiliarity with the subject) that it must be researched in greater detail than the board can presently handle. In this case try to get volunteers or (if necessary) appoint people for a special committee to pursue the question and bring back information and recommendations. Board time shouldn't be wasted trying to tackle subjects for which the group is unprepared.

To keep your meeting moving you must also be able to handle people who play negative roles in the group. George may make caustic comments that stop a discussion cold; Sandra may joke about a subject so that any action seems irrelevant; Anne may assert herself as the recognized expert, and so other opinions are squelched. You cannot change the personalities of your members, but you can largely control the situation. Arguments should be stopped if they don't clarify an issue. When allegations are made ("You environmentalists hate industry," or, "Business doesn't care if it destroys the environment"), point out that these are generalizations and "our job is to judge this specific issue strictly on its merits."

The person who puts down the rest of the group on the basis that he or she is the recognized expert should be told that, although you appreciate his expertise, everyone has had some experience with the question and should have a chance to discuss it.

If unfair accusations have been made, or logic thrown to the winds, a firm, "We don't all feel that way, Tom; Mary did you want to make a comment?" is enough to get back on the track. Some people just like to be cantankerous and sound off. In such cases the president should ask the speaker if he has a specific suggestion for board consideration. ("Wait a minute, Mike; how exactly do you want us to address this problem?" Or, "I'm not sure of your point, Mary. Are you against the whole program, or do you have a specific suggestion you want us to vote on?") Your objector may have legitimate arguments against a program, but unless he can offer a solution, it's not reasonable to permit him to spend the board's time either flailing away or philosophizing. Insist that complaints and long-winded remarks have a purpose, or are ended.

Remember, though, that there is nothing wrong with a strongly expressed statement or a heated debate from time to time if the arguments are made strictly on the merits of the issue. If you keep returning to the track and ignoring or controlling excesses, your members learn that the best way to get attention is to make real contributions.

To sum up: Meetings should be goal-oriented, but fun. The lighter the attitude and more open the discussion, the more people will feel they play a real role in the organization. They won't have fun if they don't think they are accomplishing anything, and they won't have fun if matters are dispatched with such alacrity that members aren't a part of the process. The key to *most* successful volunteer board meetings is that *people should enjoy coming*.

# Afterword

ENOUGH SAID. You now have many tools—ideas and knowledge—to do a good job. Some are tools based on my own mistakes or on the mistakes I saw others make. If they save you embarrassment and frustration and make your volunteer work easier and more fun, my purpose in writing this book has been served.

Remember that the suggestions I've made may not always work for you, and that they aren't set in concrete. In all situations, you have to decide what will work best for you, in your particular organization. Remember, too, that through no fault of your own, the best plans sometimes go terribly awry; somebody you trust may fail you at a crucial moment; machinery you depend on may break down. Because there is no way to have all the necessary knowledge and backup, you must keep a grip on reality and a good sense of humor.

Your purpose will never be the be-all and end-all of life. While it indeed may be terribly important, you must keep in mind that you weren't put on this earth to save it, only to do your best to help.

Finally, I've said it before—*have fun*! I wish I'd had this information before I started bumbling my way through the volunteer world. We all learn—in our schools and homes and jobs as well as in volunteer life—that we have to take a step at a time, learning as much as we can from others, but also knowing that much is to be learned by doing the work itself. When we miss a step and falter, we're at least assured that we'll be more aware next time, and *that* knowledge kept me going.

I hope this book has armed you with information that makes it easier to tackle your jobs with zest, inspiration and joy, as you do your part to make this a better world in which to live. That, after all, is the role of the volunteer.

# Appendix

# Organization Bylaws

**I**F YOU ARE STARTING a new organization or rewriting your old bylaws, you can get ideas by looking at the bylaws of organizations similar to your own. The bylaws I give in this section are for general guidance only. You will write your own to fit your specific needs. Keep in mind your possible need for incorporation, tax-exempt status, and the right to lobby. It is important to consult an attorney when you write your bylaws.

The suggestions I offer in this section are fairly typical for the following types of groups:

I. A nonprofit organization of individual members who share a common interest.

II. A council of *individual* members who strongly share the organization purpose; and *organization* members whose primary purposes are very diverse and some of whose individual members may not agree with the council's primary purpose.

III. A council of *individual* members and *organization members whose own members all belong to the council,* and who individually and collectively share a common bond.

**Example I:** *A typical nonprofit organization*

BYLAWS FOR THE
SOUTH POLE NEIGHBORHOOD ASSOCIATION*

As Amended by the Membership
September 1, 1981

ARTICLE I—NAME

The Name of this organization shall be the South Pole Neighborhood
Association.

ARTICLE II—PURPOSE

The purpose of this organization shall be to . . .

ARTICLE III—MEMBERSHIP

Membership shall be open to anyone subscribing to the purpose of the
Association and living within the boundaries of the South Pole. There
will be no discrimination based on race, color, creed or national origin.

ARTICLE IV—BOARD OF DIRECTORS

**Sec. 1.** The Board of Directors shall be composed of the elected four officers, who are president, vice-president, secretary and treasurer, and
eight other members.
**Sec. 2.** The directors who are not officers shall be elected for two-year
terms, half (4) to be elected each year.
**Sec. 3.** No director shall serve in the same capacity for more than two
consecutive terms.

ARTICLE V—DUTIES OF THE BOARD OF DIRECTORS

**Sec. 1.** The Board of Directors shall: Have general supervision of the
affairs of the Association; Make recommendations to the Association for
action on such items as budget, projects and proposed nonbudget
expenditures over $25.00; In the event of a vacancy in any office, fill the
vacancy for the unexpired term; Where the secretary or treasurer have
failed to provide timely reports as deemed necessary by the Board, to
name a replacement; Prepare a budget in each fiscal year and submit it
for consideration and action by the Association at the regular meeting in
September; Establish the purpose of all committees; Direct the audit of
the treasurer's records at least once annually; Perform such other duties
as may be prescribed by the membership and these bylaws.

* These bylaws are a composite of sample bylaws kindly provided me by
the firm of Mohney, Goodrich & Titta, P.C.

## ARTICLE VI—EXECUTIVE COUNCIL: OFFICERS

**Sec. 1.** The Executive Council shall be composed of the elected officers. They shall have general supervision of the Association between meetings of the Board of Directors; Approve committee chair and the assistant treasurer appointments; Authorize any persons, in addition to the treasurer, to issue and sign checks during each fiscal year.

**Sec. 2.** The officers shall be elected yearly for a term of one year and may not serve more than two consecutive years in any one office.

## ARTICLE VI—DUTIES OF THE OFFICERS

**Sec. 1.** All elected officers shall serve on the Board of Directors.

**Sec. 2.** The President shall: Preside at all meetings of the Association, Executive Council, and the Board of Directors; Vote only to break a tie, or to make a tie in order to pass a question on to the Association; Exercise general supervision over the interests and welfare of the Association; Appoint the assistant treasurer and all committee chairs as needed, subject to approval of the Executive Council; Be an ex-officio member of all committees except the nominating committee; Call all meetings of the Association, Executive Council and the Board of Directors; Perform such duties as are required by the Board of Directors, the membership and

**Sec. 3.** The Vice-President shall: Act in the absence of or during the incapacity of the President; Accept at least one other responsibility as may be agreed upon by the Vice-president and the President.

**Sec. 4.** The Secretary shall: Write and maintain minutes of all meetings of the Association, Executive Council and the Board of Directors; Provide minutes in a timely fashion to the Executive Council, Board of Directors and the Association as determined by the President; Appoint a substitute secretary when the secretary cannot perform these duties; Perform other such duties as may normally be a part of the office of the Secretary as assigned by the President or the Board of Directors.

**Sec. 5.** The Treasurer shall: Receive, account for and deposit in a bank, all funds of the Association, as directed by the Board of Directors; Make authorized disbursements by the issuance of checks which shall be countersigned by another officer; Keep an accurate record of the names and addresses of all members and dues paid; Maintain appropriate financial records which shall be subject to inspection and audit as directed by the Board of Directors. Prepare and submit such financial statements or reports as may be required by laws or regulations and/or as requested by the President, Board of Directors, or the Club; Perform such other duties as may be assigned by the President or the Board of Directors.

**Sec. 6.** The Assistant Treasurer shall: Assist the treasurer in any way practicable; Perform such other duties as may be assigned by the President or the Board of Directors.

## ARTICLE VII—COMMITTEES

**Sec. 1.** Committees shall be standing and special. Standing committees shall be 1. Newsletter; 2. Publicity; 3. Education; 4. Membership; 5. Legislation and lobbying.

**Sec. 2.** All committees shall be composed of a chairperson and at least two other members. The president shall be a member ex-officio of all committees.

**Sec. 3.** The purpose of each committee, and its duties, shall be in writing and provided to each committee chair.

**Sec. 4.** (The duties of the standing committees may be listed, as they are for the officers.)

## ARTICLE VIII—MEETINGS

**Sec. 1.** Regular meetings of the Association shall be held once a month. The June meeting shall be known as the Annual Meeting, at which time the officers and four other directors shall be elected. Special meetings of the Association may be called by the President, or at the request of the Board of Directors or at least ten Association members. The time and place of general membership meetings of the Association shall be decided by the Executive Council.

**Sec. 2.** A quorum at any meeting of the Association shall consist of the members present. Except where otherwise prescribed in the bylaws, decisions shall be made by majority vote.

**Sec. 3.** Notice for any special meeting of the Association must be provided in writing to the membership at least twenty days in advance of the meeting.

**Sec. 4.** Notice for any special meeting of the Board of Directors must be provided to the directors at least three days prior to the meeting.

**Sec. 5.** Notice for any special meeting of the Executive Council may be given at any time prior to the meeting provided there is agreement by all members of the Executive Council regarding time and place.

## ARTICLE IX—REMOVAL FROM OFFICE

Any officer may be removed from office by a 3/4 vote of the total membership of the duly elected members of the Board of Directors. Any director who is absent from three consecutive meetings of the Board may be replaced by a majority vote of the Board.

## ARTICLE X—DUES

The annual dues of the members shall be determined from year to year, the amount to be fixed by the Board of Directors at the first meeting in each fiscal year.

## ARTICLE XI—FISCAL YEAR

The fiscal year of this organization shall be from (_____) to (_____).

### ARTICLE XII—AMENDMENTS

These bylaws may be amended by a 2/3 vote of the members attending a regularly scheduled meeting of the Association, provided that the proposed amendments shall have been read at a previous meeting and submitted in writing to each member at least twenty days before the vote.

### ARTICLE XIII—DISSOLUTION

This Association may be dissolved at any time by a vote of 2/3 of the members present at a special meeting of the Association called for that purpose.

**Example II.** *A Council of individual members and organization members*

THE BYLAWS GIVEN HERE are those of an extremely effective, existing Council, the West Michigan Environmental Action Council. Unless requested by its organization members, the Action Council speaks only for its individual members. (All members, of course, are free to speak on their own behalf.) WMEAC works closely with groups and individuals who are studying various facets of an environmental problem, and then shares its information and conclusions with a broad spectrum of the public—its member organizations. Such organizations (service clubs, unions, student groups, auxiliaries, PTAs, etc.) respect, for example, the combined expertise of the League of Women Voters, various conservation groups, college professors, and an attorney's study group. The council therefore can elicit very broad interest, further study, and strong support for a cause.

BYLAWS
OF
WEST MICHIGAN ENVIRONMENTAL ACTION COUNCIL, INC.
A Michigan Nonprofit Corporation

### ARTICLE I

#### Offices

**Section 1.** *Principal and Other Offices.* The principal office of the corporation shall be located in the County of Kent, State of Michigan. The corporation may have such other offices, either within or without such

County, as the board of directors may determine or as the affairs of the corporation may require from time to time.

## ARTICLE II

### Membership and Dues

**Section 1.** *Eligibility.* Membership shall be open to all individuals and organizations concerned with the enjoyment or management of natural resources and the general and ecological welfare of our environment, which individuals and organizations subscribe to the purposes set forth in the Articles of Incorporation. The initial members may be selected by the incorporators.

**Section 2.** *Classes of Membership.* There shall be the following classes of membership:

A. Individual
   1. Regular
   2. Sustaining
   3. Patron

B. Organizational
   1. Regular
   2. Sustaining
   3. Patron

**Section 3.** *Applications for Membership.* Membership in any of the above classifications shall be by application and paying the prescribed dues for such type of membership.

**Section 4.** *Dues.*

A. The following shall be the schedule of annual dues for classes of membership:

|  | Individual | Organizational |
|---|---|---|
| Regular | $ 5.00 | $ 25.00 |
| Sustaining | 25.00 | 50.00 |
| Patron | 100.00 | 200.00 |

B. Dues shall be paid to the Treasurer at or before the Annual Meeting.

**Section 5.** *Voting Body.* Each member shall have one vote on all matters brought before the membership.

**Section 6.** *Termination of Membership.*

A. Membership may be terminated by written resignation to the Secretary of the Corporation.

B. Membership shall be automatically terminated if dues are one year in arrears.

C. Any member may have his or its membership terminated by a 2/3 vote of the Board of Directors at any time it shall consider it in the best interests of the Council.

**Section 7.** *Reinstatement of Membership.* A member may be reinstated by approval of the Board of Directors.

## ARTICLE III

### Meetings of Members

**Section 1.** *Annual Meeting.* The members shall hold an annual meeting for the election of officers and directors of the corporation and the transaction of such other business as may properly come before the meeting on the first Thursday of the month of May of each year at a time and place set by the Board of Directors. At this meeting the officers and directors shall be elected, unless the Board of Directors deems it advisable to conduct the balloting by mail prior to the Annual Meeting.

**Section 2.** *Regular Meetings.* Regular meetings of the members shall be held in September, November, January, March and May (the Annual Meeting) unless the members of the Board of Directors shall otherwise order.

**Section 3.** *Special Meetings.* Special meetings of the members may be called by the Board of Directors or at the request of at least ten members.

**Section 4.** *Notice of Meetings.* Notice for all meetings shall be given to all members at least fifteen (15) days prior thereto.

**Section 5.** *Quorum.* A quorum of any properly called and noticed meeting of members shall consist of the members present.

## ARTICLE IV

### Board of Directors

**Section 1.** *Power of Directors.* The affairs of the corporation shall be managed by its board of directors.

**Section 2.** *Number, Quorum and Tenure of Directors.* The number of directors of the corporation shall be twenty. The directors shall include the Chair, Vice Chair, Secretary and Treasurer, and sixteen (16) other persons, all of whom shall be members of the corporation or officially named delegates of organizational members. The Chair of any standing committee established by the Board of Directors shall be entitled to notice of, and to attend, all meetings of directors, but any such chairman shall not be entitled to a vote.

**Section 3.** *Term of Office.* The term of office for the nonofficer members of the Board of Directors shall be for two years, and the terms of office shall be staggered so that in any given year the terms of either seven or eight nonofficer elected directors shall expire. Nonofficer directors shall be eligible for one re-election. Each director shall hold office until his successor shall have been elected and qualified.

**Section 4.** *Quorum.* A quorum of the Board of Directors shall be seven members of the Board of Directors, provided that all directors were properly notified of the meeting.

**Section 5.** *Vacancies.* Any vacancy occurring in the Board of Directors and any directorship to be filled by reason of an increase in the number of directors shall be filled by the Board of Directors. A majority of the remaining directors, though less than a quorum, or a sole remaining director, may fill such vacancies.

**Section 6.** *Distribution of Assets.* No director or member shall possess any property right in or to the property of the corporation. In the event the corporation owns or holds any property upon its dissolution and winding up, after paying or adequately providing for its debts and obligations, the Board of Directors shall dispose of the remaining property in accordance with the provisions of the Articles of Incorporation.

**Section 7.** *Annual Meeting of Board of Directors and Regular Meetings of Directors.* The Board of Directors shall hold an annual meeting for the transaction of such business as may properly come before the meeting immediately following the annual meeting of members at a place set by the prior board of directors. Such meeting of directors shall be held without other notice than this bylaw. The Board of Directors may provide by resolution the time and place, either within or without the State of Michigan, for the holding of additional regular meetings of the Board of Directors without other notice than such resolution.

**Section 8.** *Special Meetings of Directors.* Special meetings of the Board of Directors may be called by or at the request of the chairman, or any two (2) directors. Such meetings may be held at the principal office of the corporation or any other place or places within or without the state of Michigan which may be designated in the Notice of Meeting or by the written consent of all of the directors.

**Section 9.** *Notice.* Written, telephone or personal notice of any special meeting of the Board of Directors shall be given to each director. Any written notice shall be delivered or sent to the address given by him or it to the corporation. Said notice shall be given at least twenty-four (24) hours previous to the meeting, if delivered personally or sent by telegram, and shall be given three (3) business days previous to the meeting if sent by mail. If a director has given no address to the corporation, notice shall be delivered or sent to him at the principal office of the corporation. If notice be given by telegram it shall be deemed delivered when the telegram is delivered to the telegraph company, and if mailed, such notice shall be deemed delivered when deposited in the United States mail in a sealed envelope, with postage thereon prepaid.

**Section 10.** *Waiver of Notice, Consent to Meeting or Approval of Minutes.* The transactions of any meeting of the Board of Directors, however called and noticed or wherever held, shall be as valid as though had at the meeting duly held upon notice, if a quorum is present and if, either before or after the meeting, each of the directors not present signs a written waiver of notice or a consent to holding such meeting or an approval of the minutes thereof. All such waivers, consents and approvals shall be filed with the minutes of the proceedings of the Board of Directors. Presence at any meeting of a director shall be deemed a waiver of notice and consent to holding the meeting by him.

**Section 11.** *Action by Written Consent.* Any action required or permitted to be taken by the Board of Directors may be taken without a meeting if all members of the board shall individually or collectively consent in writing to such action. Such written consent or consents shall be filed with the minutes of the proceedings of the board. Such action by written consent shall have the same force and effect as a unanimous vote of such directors. This section shall not authorize any committee of the Board of Directors to take action by written consent without a meeting.

## ARTICLE V

### Committees

**Section 1.** *Committees.* There shall be two kinds of committees — Standing and Special. The chairman shall be an ex officio member of all committees except the Nominating Committee.

**Section 2.** *Standing Committees.* The chairman shall appoint all Standing Committees subject to the approval of the Board of Directors for the term of one year. Said Standing Committees shall be: Finance; Publicity and Membership.

**Section 3.** *Special Committees.* Special Committees may be appointed as needed by the chair subject to the approval of the Board of Directors.

## ARTICLE VI

### Officers

**Section 1.** *Officers Named and Terms of Office.* The officers of this Council shall be a chairperson, vice chair, secretary and treasurer and such other officers as the members may from time to time deem necessary, and shall serve for one year. All officers may be re-elected for one additional term, or until a successor is elected.

**Section 2.** *Eligibility for Office.* Individual members and officially named delegates of organizational members shall be eligible to hold office.

**Section 3.** *Nomination and Election of Officers.*

A. Election shall be held at the Annual Meeting or by mail within one month prior to the Annual Meeting.

B. A Nominating Committee appointed by the Board of Directors shall prepare a slate of officers with at least one candidate for each office prior to the Annual Meeting.

C. Further nominations may be made from the floor at the Annual Meeting or if the balloting is done by mail, write-in nominations may be made.

D. A plurality vote shall elect.

E. Officers shall take office immediately following the Annual Meeting at which they are elected.

**Section 4.**

A. The Chair shall:

> 1. Preside at all meetings of the members and the Board of Directors.
>
> 2. Exercise general supervision over the interests and welfare of the corporation in the community.
>
> 3. Appoint all committees, standing and special, subject to the approval of the Board of Directors.
>
> 4. Be an ex-officio member of all committees, except the Nominating Committee.
>
> 5. Call all meetings of the members and of the Board of Directors.
>
> 6. Perform such other duties as normally pertain to the office of chair.

B. The Vice-Chair shall:

> 1. Act in the absence or during the incapacity of the Chair.
>
> 2. Perform duties related to organization and liaison between the corporation and other groups.
>
> 3. Perform such other duties as may be assigned by the Chair or the Board of Directors.

C. The Secretary shall:

> 1. Write and maintain the minutes of all meetings of the members and the Board of Directors.
>
> 2. Be custodian of all records and papers of the corporation except the records of the treasurer.
>
> 3. Keep an accurate record of names and addresses of all members.

4. Perform other duties which normally are a part of the office of secretary and such other duties as may be assigned by the Chairman or the Board of Directors.

D. The Treasurer shall:

1. Receive and disburse all funds of the corporation and deposit them in a bank as directed by the Board of Directors.

2. Report to the Board of Directors and the members at each meeting.

3. Provide the records for an annual audit.

4. Perform such other duties as may be assigned by the Chair or the Board of Directors.

E. The officers shall constitute the Executive Committee which shall have general supervision of the corporation's affairs between meetings of the members and board of directors.

## ARTICLE VII

### Funds and Finance

**Section 1.** *Fiscal year.* The fiscal year of the corporation shall be from April 1, to March 31.

**Section 2.** *Funds and Finance.* Revenue from sources other than dues may be raised in such manner as determined by the Board of Directors.

**Section 3.** *Authority to Borrow Funds.* The Board of Directors may, whenever the general interests of the corporation require the same, authorize the officers to borrow money and issue its promissory note or bond for the repayment thereof with or without interest, and to mortgage its property as security for its debts or other lawful engagements. The Board of Directors in authorizing any such action, shall set the particular sum, the rate of interest and the time of maturity of the loan or engagement.

**Section 4.** *Budget.* As soon as possible after the Annual Meeting, a budget of the estimated income and expenditures for the year shall be adopted by the Board of Directors.

## ARTICLE VIII

### Amendments

These bylaws may be amended by a 2/3 vote at any meeting of the members or the Board of Directors providing prior notification of the proposed amendments has been given to the members or the Board of Directors, as the case may be.

*ARTICLE IX*

*Dissolution*

This corporation may be dissolved at any time by a vote of 2/3 of the members present at a meeting of the members called for that purpose. The assets shall be distributed in accordance with the Articles of Incorporation and these bylaws.

**Example III.** *A council of individual members and organization members whose individual members all belong to the council, and who individually and collectively share a common bond.*

Such a group is the highly successful Michigan United Conservation Clubs, whose groups all share a common purpose such as outdoor recreation, and environmental protection and enhancement. This huge and well-known organization speaks for both its individual members and the individual members belonging to its member organizations. All are free to speak on their own behalf. Elected delegates from each member organization come together once a year to vote on resolutions offered by their clubs and the council's board of directors. Those resolutions, as passed, are the basis for MUCC's policy on issues. Its spokesmen, therefore, speak for a lot of people and this translates into clout at the legislative level.

MUCC has a third category of membership for organizations whose members do not want to join individually.

For a copy of their lengthy and detailed bylaws, write to MUCC and enclose $2.00 with a self-addressed manila envelope. The address is:

FIELD REPRESENTATIVE
**Michigan United Conservation Clubs**
P. O. Box 20235
Lansing, Michigan 48909

# A Short
# Bibliography

CARNEGIE, DALE. *How to Win Friends and Influence People.* New York: Simon & Schuster, 1937. Carnegie's little classic espouses a genuine understanding and appreciation of other people and offers ways to work within their limitations and perceptions. His ideas are not always as useful or applicable as he implies, but I nevertheless highly recommend it for anyone who works with other people.

GABA, PATRICIA V. AND DANIEL M. *Nonprofit Organization Handbook: A Guide to Fund Raising, Grants, Lobbying, Membership Building, Publicity and Public Relations.* Englewood Cliffs, N.J.: Prentice-Hall, 1979. Format is a large looseleaf notebook. A bit overwhelming for the average club, but full of detailed advice and information.

LONG, FERN. *All About Meetings: A Practical Guide.* Dobbs Ferry, New York: Oceana Publications, 1967. Useful information and ideas about your organization activities.

VOLUNTEER: The National Center for Citizen Involvement has a book distribution service specifically relating to volunteers. A free catalogue may be obtained from them by writing: Volunteer Readership, PO Box 1807, Boulder, Colorado, 80306. The VOLUNTEER offices in Washington can also be helpful in answering questions pertaining to voluntary organizations. Contact: VOLUNTEER, 1214 16th St. NW, Washington, D.C. 20036. Phone (202) 467-5560.

WALTERS, BARBARA. *How to Talk with Practically Anybody About Practically Anything.* Garden City, New York: Doubleday & Co., 1970. Warm advice for the times you must talk with VIPs, or any stranger.

WELCH, MARY SCOTT. *Networking: The Great New Way for Women to Get Ahead.* New York and London: Harcourt Brace Jovanovich, 1980. Although this book is addressed to a specific audience, the principles of sharing information by meeting together are presented so convincingly and usefully that I recommend it not only for career women, but for anyone working in any group.

WINSTON, STEPHANIE. *Getting Organized: The Easy Way to Put Your Life in Order.* New York: W. W. Norton & Co., 1978. How to keep personally organized, your daily tasks well managed, is usefully presented in this book.